The Basics of
Cyber Warfare

The Basics of Cyber Warfare

Understanding the Fundamentals of Cyber Warfare in Theory and Practice

Steve Winterfeld

Jason Andress

Technical Editor

Andrew Hay

AMSTERDAM • BOSTON • HEIDELBERG • LONDON
NEW YORK • OXFORD • PARIS • SAN DIEGO
SAN FRANCISCO • SINGAPORE • SYDNEY • TOKYO

ELSEVIER

Syngress is an Imprint of Elsevier

SYNGRESS,

Acquiring Editor:	*Chris Katsaropoulos*
Development Editor:	*Benjamin Rearick*
Project Manager:	*Malathi Samayan*
Designer:	*Russell Purdy*

Syngress is an imprint of Elsevier
225 Wyman Street, Waltham, MA 02451, USA

Library of Congress Cataloging-in-Publication Data
Winterfeld, Steve.
The basics of cyber warfare : understanding the fundamentals of cyber warfare in theory and practice / Steve Winterfeld, Jason Andress.
        pages cm
Includes bibliographical references and index.
ISBN 978-0-12-404737-2 (alk. paper)
1. Information warfare. 2. Computer networks–Security measures. I. Andress, Jason. II. Title.
U163.W57 2013
355.3'43–dc23

                              2012043184

British Library Cataloguing-in-Publication Data
A catalogue record for this book is available from the British Library

ISBN: 978-0-12-404737-2

Printed in the United States of America

Transferred to Digital Printing in 2014

Working together
to grow libraries in
developing countries

www.elsevier.com • www.bookaid.org

For information on all Syngress publications, visit our werbsite at *www.syngress.com*

Dedication

We thank our families and friends for their guidance, support, and fortitude through-out this project. We dedicate this book to those in the security industry who are making the world a better place through efforts like Hackers for Charity (You may have seen their T-shirts—"i hack charities." For more information, go to http://hackersforcharity.org/). To those who are not we say—get engaged!

Contents

Author Biography

Steve Winterfeld is the Chief Technology Officer (CTO) of TASC's Defense/Civil Business Group, as well as TASC's Cyber Tech Director and senior CyberWarrior instructor. During his career, he has supported a number of important cyber projects, most notably building the Computer Emergency Response Center (CERT) for US Army South, which is responsible for monitoring security in real time and conducting forensic investigations on intrusions and the developing the first Certification and Accreditation (C&A) approval for the Global Hawk Unmanned Aerial System (UAS). He holds CISSP, PMP, SANS GSEC, Six Sigma certifications in addition to an M.S. in computer information systems.

Dr. Jason Andress (ISSAP, CISSP, GPEN, CISM) is a seasoned security professional with a depth of experience in both the academic and business worlds. In his present and previous roles, he has provided information security expertise to a variety of companies operating globally. He has taught undergraduate and graduate security courses since 2005 and conducts research in the area of data protection. He has written several books and publications covering topics including data security, network security, penetration testing, and digital forensics.

Introduction

BOOK OVERVIEW AND KEY LEARNING POINTS

This book is designed as an introduction to the strategic, operational, and tactical aspects of the conflicts in cyberspace today. This book is largely a higher level view of the material in "Cyber Warfare Techniques, Tactics and Tools for Security Practitioners" published in 2011, and also includes updates regarding events that have happened since the publication of the first book.

The book shares two very different perspectives of the two authors on what many are calling cyber warfare today. One comes from a commercial background and the other brings the military viewpoint. The book is designed to help everyone understand the essentials of what is happening today, as well as provide a strong background on the issues we are facing.

This book is unique in that it provides the information in a manner that can be used to establish a strategic cybersecurity vision for an organization but it is also designed to contribute to the national debate on where cyber is going.

BOOK AUDIENCE

This book will provide a valuable resource to those involved in cyber warfare activities regardless of where their focus is; policy maker, CEO, CISO, doctrinal development, penetration testers, security professionals, network, and system administrators, or college instructors. The information provided on cyber tactics and attacks can also be used to assist in engineering with better and more efficient procedures and technical defenses.

Those in management positions will find this information useful as well, from the standpoint of developing better overall risk management strategies for their organizations. The concepts covered in this book will help determine how to allocate resources and can be used to drive security projects and policies in order to mitigate some of the larger issues discussed.

HOW THIS BOOK IS ORGANIZED

This book is designed to take the reader through a logical progression for a foundational understanding of today's cyber battlespace, but the content and organization of the topics in this book are build as standalone modules of information. It is not necessary to read the book from front to back or even in any particular order. In the areas where we refer to information located in other chapters in the book, we have endeavored to point out where the information can be found. The following descriptions will provide an overview of the contents of each chapter:

Chapter 1: Cyber Threatscape

In Chapter 1 is an overview of the cyber threatscape based on a graphical map which lays out the Methodology and Resources then shows the Attackers and Hackers that use them to beat the defenses (shown as defensive mountain range) to get to the Valuable Data. The map is intended to show the interaction and complexity across the cyber domain. The hacker's methodology, tools, and processes listed are generally the same ones used by security professionals; though the security professional has (written) authorization to conduct attacks and operations.

Chapter 2: Military Doctrine

In Chapter 2 we discuss how the concept of what a war means is changing and examine whether we are in a cyber war today. We discuss the differences between conventional and cyber wars and how conventional warfare is a poor standard against which to measure its cyber equivalent. How a cyber war, whether strictly cyber in nature or in combination with traditional war, could lead to an international disaster, changing economies, enabling an increased cyber crime wave, and facilitating unprecedented espionage. We cover the traditional war-fighting domains of land, sea, air, and space both as they relate to cyber operations and what we can learn from them as cyber becomes more mature as the fifth war-fighting domain. We also review the different threats, the impacts they are having, and what their motivations might be.

Chapter 3: Cyber Doctrine

In Chapter 3 explores the state of current cyber warfare doctrine on both the nation state and military. We discuss how every country with a dependence on IT infrastructure is developing strategies and capabilities to protect and exercise national power and examined some of the traditional tactics and products that the military needs to adapt to the cyberspace environment. We also cover some of the directives used by federal agencies and governments to guide behavior in this virtual environment. Finally we look at how organizations are training both to develop new doctrine and execute their current plans.

Chapter 4: Cyber Tools and Techniques

In Chapter 4 we discuss the various tools that we might use in conducting Computer Network Operations (CNO), and the methods that we might use to defend against an attacker using them. We discuss the tools used for reconnaissance, access and privilege escalation, exfiltration, sustaining our connection to a compromised system, assault tools, and obfuscation tools, many of which are free, or have free versions, and are available to the general public. We cover the intersection of the physical and logical realms and how making changes to either realm can affect the other, sometimes to a disastrous extent. Additionally we cover supply chain concerns and the potential consequences of corruption or disruption in the supply chain.

Chapter 5: Offensive Tactics and Procedures

In Chapter 5 we discuss the basics of Computer Network Exploitation (CNE) and Computer Network Attack (CNA). We explain that exploitation in this context means reconnaissance or espionage, and then discuss how it is conducted. We cover identifying our targets in the sense of both gleaning information from targets of attacks and in the sense of identifying targets to be surveilled. We talk about the different factors involved in cyber warfare, including the physical, logical, and electronic elements of warfare. We also discussed the different phases of the attack process: reconnaissance, scanning, accessing systems, escalating privileges, exfiltrating data, assaulting the system, sustaining our access, and obfuscating any traces that might be left behind. We compare how this parallels and differs from typical hacker attacks.

Chapter 6: Psychological Weapons/Social Engineering

In Chapter 6 we cover social engineering and discuss how it can be a dangerous threat vector to all organizations and individuals. We look at this from a military mindset and pull lessons from how they conduct interrogations and conduct counter-intelligence. We talk about how the security policies, culture, and training must be reinforced often to insure the work force stays vigilant and how a great technical security infrastructure can be subverted by just going after the people.

Chapter 7: Defensive Tactics and Procedures

In Chapter 7 we discuss Computer Network Defense (CND). We talk about what exactly it is that we attempt to secure, in the sense of data and information as well as security awareness and training efforts in order to mitigate what sometimes is the weakest link in our defenses, this is being authorized by normal users. We also present some of the different strategies that we recommend be used to defend ourselves against attack.

Chapter 8: Challenges We Face

We define the 30 key issues that are impacting cybersecurity and map how they should be categorized. We then break them out into levels of difficulty and resources required to solve. We also discuss how they are interrelated. Finally we look at both who and how they should be addressed, to include rough timelines on when they might be resolved.

Chapter 9: The Future of Technology and Their Impacts on Cyber Warfare

As we look to what lies ahead we examine the logical evolution based on current cybersecurity technology and trends. A review of some of the technology based trends that will have the greatest influence on cyber warfare as well as the policy based development that could have the most impact will provide a basis to look at what could happen. We also cover some of the best ways to defend in today's contested virtual environment.

Appendix: Cyber Timeline

We have also included an Appendix with a timeline of the major events that have impacted or driven the conflicts in cyberspace.

CONCLUSION

Writing this book was a true journey. A considerable amount of debate among all those involved in the book took place over what would build the best foundation to address the subject, but in the end a solid balance was struck between the broad perspective and specific practical techniques. The hope is that this book will both contribute to the national discussion on where cyberspace is headed and what role each one of us can play.

Cyber Threatscape

INFORMATION IN THIS CHAPTER:

- How Did We Get Here?
- Attack Methodology Plus Tools/Techniques Used
- Attackers (The Types of Threats)
- How Most Organizations Defend Today (Defensive Mountain Range)?
- Targeted Capabilities (What We should be Defending)

HOW DID WE GET HERE?

In the early 1980s, when ARPANET was becoming the World Wide Web which grew into today's Internet, the focus was on interoperability and reliability as a means of communication and potential command and control in the event of an emergency. Everyone with access to the system knew each other and security was not a consideration. Then, in the late 1980s, trouble started; Robert Morris released the first worm (a self-replicating piece of malware) and Clifford Stoll discovered Soviet Block spies stealing US secrets via a mainframe at the University of California, Berkeley. These were quickly followed by a number of incidents that highlighted the security risks associated with our new communication capability (see Appendix 1 for list of major events through the years).

The key events as they relate to and impact the military occurred in the mid-to late-1990s when Time magazine had a cover on "Cyber War." The 1998 Solar Sunrise incident hit the news as the Pentagon got hacked while America was at war with Iraq, but the instigators were two kids from California. Moonlight Maze, where the Department of Defense (DoD) found intrusions from systems in the Soviet Union (though the source of the attacks was never proven) and Russia denied any involvement (hackers will often route their attacks through countries that will not cooperate with an investigation). By the early 2000s, a series of attacks, generally accepted as being from China, were identified and code named Titan Rain. The name was changed to Byzantine Hades after the Titan Rain code name was disclosed in the media and changed again when the Byzantine Hades code name was posted to

> **NOTE**
>
> Code Word/Name—A word or a phrase designed to represent a program or activity while remaining inconspicuous to people not cleared for the information. A code word should be assigned randomly and have no association with the program or activity it represents. Active code words are classified. If the code word/name is compromised it is cancelled and a new code word/name is issued.

WikiLeaks. The term "Advance Persistent Threat (APT)" has become the common reference term for this state-sponsored systematic electronic reconnaissance/digital espionage. By late 2000s there was a physical aspect added to the entropic attacks which the DoD code named Operation Buckshot Yankee. Thumb drives used by US Military were found to have malcode embedded which caused DoD to ban thumb drive usage on all military networks and systems.

In addition to attacks on the US Military, some international incidents occurred in the 2000s. In 2007, hackers believed to be linked to the Russian government brought down the Web sites of Estonia's parliament, banks, ministries, newspapers, and broadcasters. Estonia called on the NATO treaty for protection and troops to help recover. A year later cyber attackers hijacked government and commercial Web sites in Georgia during a military conflict with Russia, creating a new form of digital signal jamming over the Web. Finally in 2010, the Stuxnet worm attacked the systems that control Iran's nuclear material development causing damage to these systems.

There are some other key events that parallel the military's pains. In 2009, reports revealed that hackers downloaded data from the DoDs multibillion-dollar F-35 Joint Strike Fighter program, showing that the cyber attackers were going after defense contractors as well as the military itself. Then in 2010, Operation Aurora broke into the news when Google publicly revealed itself as being one of many commercial companies hacked by the APT showing that the cyber attackers were also going after commercial intellectual property. There were two troubling attacks in 2011. The first was a series of hacks exposed in the global energy report "Night Dragon" which showed how China was trying to gain a competitive edge in the energy market through espionage. The second was the RSA attack where stolen information would allow a hacker to replicate the number that showed up on the password token many organizations used to secure their networks, showing that the enemy was willing to attack the infrastructure used to protect the US.

For 30 years, there has been a continuous battle between defenders and attackers from networks around the globe. In many cases it does not matter to the attacker if the target is military, government, or commercial, they are just after as many systems as they can acquire. As new solutions are invented, new attacks are developed, and the cycle continues.

The threatscape map in Figure 1.1 was designed to assist everyone in understanding this complex environment. Some will see the map of Mordor from J.R. Tolkien's fictional Middle-Earth while others see the Ponderosa, but the map is really designed to show the methodology (upper left) and resources (lower left) the attackers (second column) will use to attempt to beat the defenses built into the mountain range (center) to get to the valuable data they want on the far side (far right side).

ATTACK METHODOLOGY PLUS TOOLS/TECHNIQUES USED

As we examine how networks are broken into, it is evident that the basic steps in the process are analogous to traditional military attack/defend doctrine. When we look at how defending armies build defense in depth, we see the same term used by network administrators—Demilitarized Zone (DMZ), just like the physical zone between South and North Korea. On the attacking side attackers go through the reconnaissance, marshal forces at the point of weakness, attack and exploit penetration to gain control over the enemy.

The major difference between Kinetic (real world) and Non-Kinetic (virtual world) warfare methodology is the weapons vs. software programs they use. So we will walk through the steps and define a few of the tools used. The tools will be covered in more detail in later chapters so this will just be to gain an initial understanding.

Attack methodology is the process or general steps used to attack a target and potential tools/techniques that can be used to conduct the attack. The major steps are recon, attack, and exploit. These steps can be a variety of activities, from launching machine to machine attacks to using social engineering. (Think of social engineering as scamming or conning someone out of information that allows the hacker to compromise a network.) Each of these steps or phases have a number of substeps to accomplish them and in many cases different hackers will both modify and automate them to suit their style.

To begin the recon phase a target is required. The target can be the specific systems that will be attacked or the personnel that use them. To attack the machines the unique Internet Protocol (IP) address for the machine or Uniform Resource Locator (URL) for the Web page must be known. To attack via the users, a phone number is generally all that is needed. IP addresses and phone numbers can be found with a quick Google search or with services like American Registry for Internet Numbers (ARIN) searches. Much of what is needed for a social engineering attack can be found on a business card.

Once the target is identified the recon begins to find the weak point or vulnerability. The attack can be against the operating system or one of the applications on it (i.e. Adobe Flash, Microsoft Office, Games, Web browsers, or an instant messenger). A scanner is run against the system to determine and list many of the vulnerabilities. Some of the more popular scanners are Nmap, Nessus, eEye Retina, and Saintscanner. Attack framework tools are available that both scan and then have the exploits to launch the attack matching vulnerabilities found built into the application.

WARNING

The only difference between a hacker tool and a cybersecurity professional tool is "written permission." Please don't load a password cracker on a work computer to test the security without permission—many people have been fired for using these tools with good intentions.

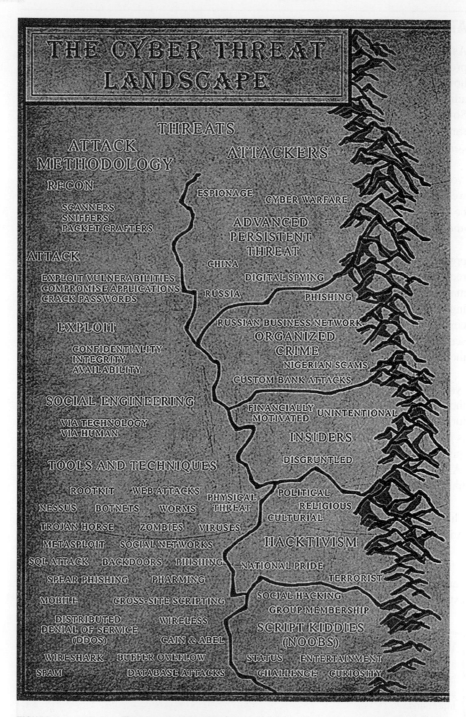

FIGURE 1.1 This is a Threatscape Map Designed to Show the Different Components in the Cyber Environment and How They Interact

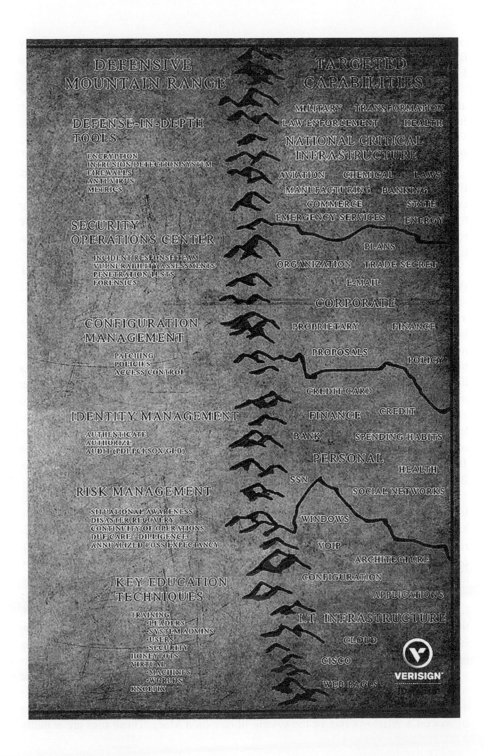

Some popular framework tools are Metasploit, Canvas, and Core Impact. Finally there is a tool that transforms a machine into a Linux system by booting off of a Linux live CD. The most popular live CD attack tool is BackTrack.

Another tool that is useful during recon is a sniffer. This is a tool that has the attacker's system mimic every computer on the network so it gets a copy of all the traffic. It will allow the attacker to read all unencrypted emails and documents as well as see the Web pages being accessed by everyone on the network. Popular sniffers are Wireshark, Ettercap, and Tcpdump. On the wireless side tools include Aircrack-ng and Kismet.

While there are a lot of recon tools that are very powerful and easy to use, the one set of tools that show how the threat environment has evolved is packet crafters. Someone with no programming skills can now craft unique attacks. Popular tools include NetCat and Hping. There are a host of other tools for recon but these represent the baseline tools used to discover the vulnerabilities that allow movement to the attack phase.

When attacking a system there are many types of malcode that can be used. At the code level there are worms or viruses that can use attack vectors like cross-site scripting (XSS) or buffer overflows to install rootkits or a Trojan horse which acts as a backdoor into a system, and is use to spread the attack. A worm spreads without any help. It infects a system and use it to find more systems to spread to, while a virus needs some user interaction like opening any type of file (email, document, presentation) or starting a program (game, video, new app). Worms and viruses use techniques like cross-site scripting or buffer overflows which attack mistakes in the code in order to compromise it. Cross-site scripting is a Web-based attack that allows unauthorized code to be executed on the viewer's computer that could result in information being stolen or the system's identification certificates being stolen. An overly simplified example of a buffer overflow is when a program asks for a phone number rather than give it the 10 digits needed the software sends 1000 digits then a command to install the malcode. Because the program does not have good error handling, it executes the malcode.

A rootkit is a program that takes over control of the operating system and tells lies about what is happening on the system. Once a rootkit is installed, it can hide the hacker's folders (i.e. hacker tools, illegal movies, stolen credit card numbers), misdirect applications (i.e. show the antivirus updating daily but don't allow it to update), or misrepresent the system status (i.e. leave port 666 open so the hacker can remotely access the system but show it as closed).

The first generation of rootkits was much like my daughter when she was four (called the fibbing 4s because that is when most kids learn to lie). Like a 4 year old, the rootkits of the first generation did not lie very well. The generation we are on now is more like when she was 21 (she was MUCH better at telling a coherent story that is not easy to detect as a lie). The current generation of rootkits does a much better job of hiding themselves from detection. The next generation will be like someone with a masters in social engineering, almost undetectable. A Trojan horse backdoor is a program that masquerades as a legitimate file (often a system file: i.e. files ending in .sys on a Windows box or the system library on a Mac). These files are actually fakes and have replaced the actual system file. The new file both runs the system and opens a backdoor to the system allowing the hacker remote control of the system.

One use for worms and viruses is to build botnet armies. A bot (also called a zombie) is a computer that is a slave to a controller. Once someone builds an army of millions of bots they can cause a distributed denial of service (DDoS) by having all of the bots try to connect to the same site or system simultaneously. This can be done to blackmail a Website (pay or be blocked so no customers can get access), disrupt command and control systems, click fraud (if Acme.org gets paid one cent for every customer that clicks on link taking them to Selling.com a botnet could be used to do that millions of times a day) or compile complex problems (much like a distributed supercomputer).

There are a number of ways to launch attacks targeted at a specific system rather than the broad net a worm or virus would catch. The attack framework tools mentioned earlier are the most common. The key is to correlate the exploit to the vulnerability. Much like there has never been a bank built that cannot be robbed, there is not a computer or network that cannot be broken into given enough resources and persistence. If no vulnerability can be found then the attacker can go after the authentication via password or credential attacks.

Cracking passwords can be done with brute force by having a program try every possible password iteration. This can be time consuming and is easy to detect but, depending on the strength of the password, is very effective. If the hacker can get access to the password file then tools like Cain & Able or Jack the Ripper can be utilized to crack them. Another technique that is available is called rainbow tables. These are databases where popular password encryption protocols have been run on every possible key combination on a standard keyboard. This precompiled list allows a simple lookup when the hacker gets access to the list of encrypted passwords. Many of these tables have done every combination for 8–20 characters and the length grows as hackers continue to use botnet to build the tables.

The exploit phase is where the attacker takes advantage of gaining control. There are generally three factors that the hacker can compromise: Confidentiality, Integrity, or Availability (CIA). When attacking confidentiality they are simply stealing secrets. Integrity attacks are when they change the data on the system. In a commercial setting this could be changing prices or customer data. On a military network it might be to change the equations used to calculate command and control guidance. Availability attacks are normally time based and can be accomplished by taking the system down or overwhelming the bandwidth. The type of exploit is based on the motivations of the attacker. They can use the system to attack more systems on the

NOTE

Exploit has three meanings within the cyber community. When talking about code it refers to malcode that allows a system to be compromised. When talking about the methodology it refers to what the payload of the attack is intended to accomplish. When talking about military doctrine it is used by the intelligence community to refer to recon/espionage.

network, misrepresent the user (send fake emails), or load a rootkit with a backdoor to maintain long-term access. They will often try to avoid detection and might even use anti-forensic techniques like log wiping and time stomping. Some will patch the system so others will not be able to break in and take it away from them. Finally they may load digital tripwire alarms to tell them if they have been detected.

Another vector of attack is social engineering. This can be done in person but is normally done over the phone. It can include research via an organization's Web site, social media, and meeting people at places like a conference to exchange business cards. The most common attack today is via email. This kind of social engineering attack is called phishing (sending general email to multiple people), spear phishing (targeted at a specific person), or whaling (targeting a specific senior member of the organization). There are also technical tools like the "Social Engineer Toolkit" that are designed to assist attacking the workforce.

ATTACKERS (THE TYPES OF THREATS)

This section will focus on the different categories of attackers. As we look at the threatscape map (Figure 1.1) the attackers not ranked or ordered in any particular way. It is important to note that while there are solid lines between them they can overlap and mix. The Advanced Persistent Threat (APT) can buy exploits from criminal elements, noobs can join hacktivist causes and, one particularly troubling paradigm shift that has happened recently, hacktivists can behave like insider threats as they steal information and then publish the stolen information on the Web sites like WikiLeaks.

APT is one of the key drivers of cyber warfare. The term APT is often used in different ways by the media, but, for purposes of this book, APT means state guided attacks. It is truly digital spying or espionage in the virtual world. Some of the most commonly referenced activities were discussed earlier (Titan Rain, Operation Buckshot Yankee, Aurora, Stuxnet, and Night Dragon). Today the US talks about the "War on Drugs" or the "Global War on Terror." These activities are very reminiscent of the Cold War era. There are also political references to economic warfare, which may be more appropriate to these activities. China or Russia are frequently named in associate with attacks, but it is important to remember that the cost of entry makes cyber war type activities attractive to all nations. There is a low cost of entry and a low risk of any significant consequences.

Organized crime on the Internet is the next topic. One of the most often joked about scams on the Internet is the "Nigerian royalty that just needs access to your bank account" scam that sends phishing emails designed to steal identities and access the victims' bank accounts. The text of the emails from the Nigerian scams will talk about how they have money that they need to get out of the country and all they need is to transfer the money to a US bank, but to do that they need access to the victim's account. These scams have been around long before the Internet but have become much easier to do in bulk and with little risk of incarceration, as the perpetrators are usually overseas. Another popular scam is selling fake medicine.

While some of the sites are selling legitimate drugs most will send fake medicine if they send anything at all. These same scams can be used to get members of the military or national security infrastructure to get involved in activities they would not do in the real world.

One of the more well-known criminal organizations is called the Russian Business Network (RBN) or Russian Mob (note this is not one single organization). If someone graduates from a university in one of the old Soviet Union block countries with a degree in computer science one of the better paying jobs is with the RBN. There they will work full time to build custom exploits targeting specific financial institutions, building botnet armies, running identity theft networks, or any one of a hundred "business ventures" for them. These organizations are staffed in one country, use systems hosted in a different country (for a while they were using systems in China) and committing crimes against citizens in a third country so it is very complex to prosecute if they are discovered. While the RBN is a good example, there are also some books on the subject like "Fatal System Error" by Joseph Menn. Russia is not the only country that has cyber-based criminal organizations; in fact the US has exposed similar activities.

You will find in many reports the rule of thumb that insider threats represent 20% of the threat but could cause 80% of the damage (recent studies show the real numbers of insiders are closer to 50%). The reason is the insiders understand what is valuable on the network and often have legitimate access to it. The three basic categories of insiders are: disgruntled employees, financially motivated (thieves), and unintentional users. Disgruntled employees can cause problems by publishing information on the Web to competitors or to fellow employees. They could also install a logic bomb that will cause damage if they stop working at the company (i.e. if Winterfeld does not show up on the employee payroll, reformat all servers in the data room). Financially motivated insiders will misuse the company assets or manipulate the system to steal. Users will also unintentionally delete files causing loss of work or might accidentally post classified documents on unclassified systems causing what is known as a spill. Spills could require destruction of the system and a lengthy investigation.

Hacktivists can be motivated by political views, cultural/religious beliefs, national pride, or terrorist ideology. The most recent example has been from a group called Anonymous. This group of loosely affiliated hackers from around the world banded together to attack organizations they felt were in the wrong. This cyber vigilante group attacked the Church of Scientology under project name Chanology in 2008 and started using their trademark saying "We are Anonymous. We are Legion. We do not forgive. We do not forget. Expect us" [1]. They have attacked MasterCard for stopping support of WikiLeaks, Law Enforcement Agencies for policy they do not support, political parties, HBGary Federal (in response to statement made by Aaron Barr), Sony (in response to a law suit they brought), the Bay Area Rapid Transit system (in response to their closing down cell phone tower coverage at the stations to prevent a protest), porn sites, and many government sites around the world. Their supporters can often be seen wearing Guy Fawkes masks from the movie "V for Vendetta." As of early 2012, the FBI has arrested many of the leaders of Anonymous, but expect more groups like this to sprout up.

Script kiddies or noobs (for new to hacker) are pejorative terms for the less skilled hackers. These are the folks who can only use the tools that can be found on the Internet. There are many different motivations to start hacking. Some are looking for a social experience and will try to join a hacker group (some groups will require proof of hacking ability before they grant membership), others enjoy the challenge or want to gain status across the hacker community, still others do it out of curiosity and think of it as entertainment. We can see many examples of these at hacker conferences like DEFCON, ShmooCon, or HOPE. The problem these script kiddies pose to the cyber warfare landscape is the amount of activity they produce. If there are millions of attacks a week launched by noobs every week, how can the APT or specific criminal activity be located? It is also important to understand that the tools they use are very powerful and they will end up PWNing (slang for own) systems. The age old adage "the defender has to get it right every time while the attacker only has to get it right once" applies here as the Defense Information Systems Agency (DISA) has consistently said the majority of systems compromised were from known exploits that could have been prevented if the systems were fully patched and configured to standard [2].

HOW MOST ORGANIZATIONS DEFEND TODAY (DEFENSIVE MOUNTAIN RANGE)?

On the threatscape map (Figure 1.1) the Defensive Mountain Range shows many of the different ways used to protect networks today. It covers the infrastructure and processes used to secure the systems and detect any intrusions. Much like real-world defenses, they need to be constantly validated, monitored, and updated.

Defense-In-Depth or multiple layers of protection is how most networks are protected today. The issue is there are so many mobile systems (laptops, phones, tablets) and removable storage devices that it is becoming increasing difficult to keep all the systems inside the defensive perimeter. Some of the critical tools are firewalls to block the attacks, intrusion detection systems (IDS) to alert on attacks, antivirus to kill the attacks that got through, and encryption of the data on the device so if the device is lost or stolen the information is still secure. The critical process needed is good security metrics. Metrics revolve around the need to quantify the impact of cyber events. They should support both the technical and senior leadership's ability to make decisions to protect the network and react to changes in risk assessment as well as support understanding of return on investment of security infrastructure. There has been a lot of work done, but there is no clear set of industry standard cyber metrics today. There are three basic types of metrics:

* *Technical:* Based on infrastructure and the incident response cycle.
* *Security return on investment (ROI):* Cost-based analysis on benefits from implementing new technology or policies. These goals must be set before they change and methods to track performance are established.
* *Risk posture:* Analysis on impact of cyber events/incidents to enterprise and operations.

> **TIP**
>
> A forensics expert is a must-have team member, but, as they can be expensive, many organizations have someone they can call on demand as opposed to having a full time staff member. The forensics expert should be called if there is any possibility of a lawsuit, human resource action (firing), or prosecution of the hacker. There must be clear policies on when they are called because, much like a real crime scene, the more people that have accessed the data the more the crime scene is compromised. The military is slowly moving toward gathering evidence in a way that it can be presented in court as opposed to just getting the systems back on line quickly.

Next comes the cell that monitors the network, usually called the Security Operations Centers (SOC) or Computer Emergency Response Team (CERT). These cells typically contain the Incident Response Teams responsible for the response cycle—Protect, Detect, React, and Recover. This is very similar to the military OODA Loop (Observe, Orient, Decide, and Act). The SOC would also be responsible for conducting Vulnerability Assessments (VA) and Penetration Tests (PT). The VA is designed to look for vulnerabilities on the network then prioritize how to fix or mitigate them. The PT is designed to test the team's ability to respond to an intrusion. Penetration Tests can also be called Red Teaming depending on the scope and interaction of the two sides. The PT team will not only find the vulnerability but exploit it and once they break in will either grab a predetermined file (called the flag) or load a file on the system (called the golden nugget). Then the SOC team must determine how the PT broke in and what they did. This will validate the team's processes and tools. One key capability that is needed after an intrusion is the forensics expert. This is someone that understands the rules of evidence and can testify in court. This analysis is key to understand what happened to prevent it from reoccurring.

Configuration Management is a critical part of the defense. A well-configured and managed network is more secure. Think of walking up to a cruise liner to start your vacation only to find it is so covered in rust you cannot tell what color it use to be painted. Common sense would prevent you from getting on. Yet because we cannot see that our network devices are past their maintenance lifecycle we put our most valuable information on the equivalent servers. The basics require timely patching. Patches must be tested before they were installed on critical operational systems so the challenge is how much time is allowed for analysis (some say 72 h but that can be expensive so there is a broad range). Well understood and enforced policies for both the users and network administrators are a must. They both can impact the security baseline with decisions on operations or processes but often do not examine the impact to security risks. Finally, access control must be managed so that only the people with a need are allowed to access the mission critical data. This can be done physically or through electronic policies. This is called the principle of least privilege and has been used for decades in the intelligence community.

Identity Management is one area that will help as users become more mobile. The three vital factors are authentication, authorization, and audit/compliance. Before someone logs into the system they should have to prove who they are with something they know (user name and password), something they have (electronic token), and/or something they do (biometrics, i.e. scan a fingerprint): this is authentication. Next they should be categorized by what kind of information they should have access to. The military uses Unclassified/Secret/Top Secret but there are a number of organizations that have designed their own system. Finally, as was mentioned earlier, as every network will have a weakness over time it is prudent to assume that someone has penetrated the network and conduct audits to find them.

Compliance is based on the legal or regulatory requirements of the industry. Some examples are: Healthcare = Health Insurance Portability and Accountability Act (HIPAA), Finance = Gramm-Leach-Bliley Act, Publicly traded companies = Sarbanes-Oxley Act, Credit Cards = Payment Card Industry, Energy Providers = North American Electric Reliability Corporation (NERC) Critical Infrastructure Protection (CIP) program, Federal agencies = Federal Information Security Management Act (FISMA), US Intelligence Community (IC) = Director of Central Intelligence Directive (DCID) 6/3, and US Military = DoD Information Assurance Certification and Accreditation Process (DIACAP). Today most of these are based on annual reviews of the systems but they are moving to real-time monitoring.

Risk Management is what all these regulations have been driving to. The goal is to achieve Situational Awareness (SA). SA is the correlation and fusion of data from multiple sources that enable decision making. Ideally it will be presented visually through a Common Operational Pictures (COP) that will facilitate true risk posture understanding and provide information in a format that enables decisions. If the network is lost then the Disaster Recovery (DR) and Continuity of Operations Plans (COOP) come into play. DR focuses on getting the network back up while the COOP is the plan to continue operations without any automation.

As we design systems and networks it is important to understand there are legal expectations of how the network will be protected. These principles are known as due care and due diligence. These should be based on the "Annualized Loss Expectancy" calculations (Vulnerability × Threat × Asset Value = Total Risk then Total Risk × Countermeasures = Residual Risk). This will help determine where the organization is in the security lifecycle: requirements definition—design and develop the protective measures, implement, and validate the defensive solution—operation maintain risk management controls. This will also allow security to be designed into the system rather that bolted on afterwards, something that is always more expensive and less effective.

One of the most effective protection techniques is education designed to alter the users' behaviors. The training must be targeted at the different types of users: leaders need to know how to manage cyber risk, system admins must understand the importance of configuration management and patching, general users need to understand how their behaviors can become vulnerabilities that hackers can exploit, and the cyber security team needs to understand the latest threats and protection tools/techniques. Some useful tools are honeypots, virtual machines, virtual worlds, and live CDs. Honeypots are systems that are deployed with no operational function so any interaction with them causes an investigation. If we install a server with data labeled "senior leaders evaluations and important financial data" it will attract insiders and hackers but as soon as they touch it the Security Operation Center (SOC) will be alerted and quickly react. Virtual Machines (VM) are software-based computers that allow anyone to simulate multiple computers with various operating systems on their computer. This allows them to test hacking from one VM to another. Virtual worlds can be used to conduct training with no travel costs. A popular business oriented virtual world is Second life. Finally to boot your current computer as a Linux machine to use some of the tools we have discussed, use a live CD like BackTrack.

TARGETED CAPABILITIES (WHAT WE SHOULD BE DEFENDING)

Targeted Capabilities break out the variety of systems, types of information and industries that the enemy is trying to compromise. The major categories are National Critical Infrastructure, Corporate, Personal, and Information Technology Infrastructure. Critical infrastructure often has aspects of the other categories embedded within it. Corporate information will normally have personal and Information Technology Infrastructure embedded.

National Critical Infrastructure Protection (CIP) includes: Banking, Law Enforcement, Laws/Legal System, Transportation, Health, Military, Chemical, Energy, State, Emergency Services, Plans, Manufacturing, Commerce, and Aviation. If any of these were not available for even short periods of time, there would be major impacts. The loss of faith in the security of aviation after the 9/11 attacks had secondary economic impacts. The loss of belief in the integrity of our financial systems could cause a run on the banks. If the power grid were to be taken down it would cause both economic and heath impacts. The issue is that most of this critical infrastructure is managed by commercial companies that have to balance risk against profit.

Corporate assets such as email accounts, proprietary info/trade secrets, finance records, policy, proposals, and organizational decisions are all of value to the competition. Depending on the nature of the information nation states, criminal organizations, hacktivists, and insiders could all be after different parts of the company.

Personal data like health records and financial information (banking and credit card accounts) are high value targets for insurance companies, criminals, espionage targets, and your personal enemies. If someone wants to target a senior member of the US Military today, finding out as much about the person on the Internet would be the first step. The same could be true of Law Enforcement Agencies that focus on the drug trade. The digital natives are putting more and more personal information on the Web. This information all ties back to two major issues: identity theft and social engineering.

Information Technology (IT) infrastructure is a target for two reasons. Hackers may want to use the infrastructure for themselves (i.e. building a botnet) or they want to know what operating systems (Windows/OS X) and network devices (VoIP, applications, specific Cisco devices) are available to allow them to find vulnerabilities. Understanding the architecture or mapping the Web pages could provide insight into how to gain unauthorized access.

SUMMARY

This has been an overview of the threatscape coving the methodology, tools, and techniques used by the different types of attackers and a review of the key parts of the defensive infrastructure employed to protect our systems as well as the general categories of information the hackers are after. These will all be covered in more detail in subsequent chapters but this foundation is intended to help tie it all together. Chapter 8 is designed to give an overview of the cyber environment, focused on the challenges. It breaks out the problems in a way that they can be evaluated against each other and facilitates a discussion on prioritization and resource allocation.

The question most often asked after discussing this cyber threatscape is how someone should protect themselves at home. The answer is "safe behaviors!" The basics go a long way such as a firewall, up-to-date antivirus, patching all applications, keeping private and financial data on a removable hard drive that is only connected when in use, and BACK UP valuable data to a place that will not be destroyed if the system is stolen or destroyed. All are mandatory for basic security, but they can all be defeated by poor security practices such as weak passwords, surfing sites known to be hot spots for malcode, opening emails or accepting invites on social networking sites from someone unknown. While there is no such thing as "security through obscurity" we should strive to not be the "low hanging fruit" that is easily PWNed.

REFERENCES

[1] Anonymous. UNK [Online]. <http://anonymousarmy.webs.com/>.
[2] Patterson BG LaWarren. Brief on operating, maintaining and defending the Army's global network enterprise. In: Cyberspace symposium, Colorado Springs; 2010.

Cyberspace Battlefield Operations

INFORMATION IN THIS CHAPTER:

- What is Cyber Warfare?
- Cyber War—Hype or Reality
- Boundaries in Cyber Warfare
- Where Cyber Fits in the War-fighting Domains

We are constantly bombarded with news about Internet events today. Cyber crime is up, watch out for the latest phishing attack trying to steal our identity, update our antivirus to avoid infection, patch the operating system to avoid a hacker taking control, new zero day attack against smartphones, Facebook privacy compromised, someone took down Twitter, and now we are hearing about cyber war.

When establishing the boundaries of the battlefield in the physical world it is usually straightforward. When two countries go to war there is a battlefront established between the two armies where active combat occurs. Wars are normally fought over land, and typically on the very land the countries are fighting for but in the current war on terrorism the reasons and boundaries are more less defined, with no set battlefront where the forces clash but instead distributed forces with no formal rank structure or doctrine but rather groups conducting guerrilla or asymmetric warfare.

Still even in unconventional warfare the two sides must operate within the same geographical area, in cyberspace the traditional boundaries disappear.

WHAT IS CYBER WARFARE?

America's information dominance tools, which helped win the Cold War, have become its Achilles heel of the cyber conflict we are in today. Our technology was far ahead of any competitor nation and we out spent them to keep the edge. Today we are more dependent on this technology than ever before, most of which is now available to our partners, competitors, and adversaries. At the same time the cost of entry into this arms cyber race is incredibly low. Furthermore the benefits of attacking someone in cyberspace far outweigh the dangers. This has lead to what many are calling a cyber war.

Definition for Cyber Warfare

A definition of cyber warfare is not easy to establish. In fact definitions for cyber and warfare are both under debate. We will start with a simple definition of cyber or cyberspace. For the purpose of this chapter we will frame the definition in the context of military environments.

Department of Defense (DoD) Joint Publication 3-13 Information Operations February 13, 2006 (Figure 2.1) defines cyberspace as the notional environment in which digitized information is communicated over computer networks [1].

The National Military Strategy for Cyberspace Operations defines cyberspace as "the domain characterized by the use of electronics and the electromagnetic spectrum to store, modify, and exchange data via networked systems and associated physical infrastructures [2]."

DoD Joint Publication 3.0 Joint Operations September 17, 2006 Incorporating Change 2, March 22, 2010 defines cyberspace as a global domain within the information environment. It consists of the interdependent network of information technology infrastructures, including the Internet, telecommunications networks, computer

FIGURE 2.1 Cyber or Computer Network Operations Fall Under this US Joint Publication Doctrinal Manual JP 3-13 for Information Operations [2]

systems, and embedded processors and controllers. Within cyberspace, electronics, and the electromagnetic spectrum are used to store, modify, and exchange data via networked systems. Cyberspace operations employ cyberspace capabilities primarily to achieve objectives in or through cyberspace. Such operations include computer network operations and activities to operate and defend the Global Information Grid [2].

United Nations (UN) definition of cyber—The global system of systems of internetted computers, communications infrastructures, online conferencing entities, databases, and information utilities generally known as the Net. This mostly means the Internet; but the term may also be used to refer to the specific, bounded electronic information environment of a corporation or of a military, government, or other organization [3].

For a definition of warfare we cannot turn to an authoritative source. The United Nations (UN) does not have a definition, so we will default to the two historical standards for military doctrine: *On War*, the exhaustive work documenting tactics during the Napoleonic War period in 1873 and *The Art of War* a more condensed version of how to conduct warfare composed in 6th century BC China.

> *ON WAR—We shall not enter into any of the abstruse definitions of war used by publicists. We shall keep to the element of the thing itself, to a duel. War is nothing but a duel on an extensive scale. If we would conceive as a unit the countless number of duels which make up a war, we shall do so best by supposing to ourselves two wrestlers. Each strives by physical force to compel the other to submit to his will: his first object is to throw his adversary, and thus to render him incapable of further resistance. War therefore is an act of violence to compel our opponent to fulfill our will [4].*

> *ART OF WAR—The art of war is of vital importance to the State. It is a matter of life and death, a road either to safety or to ruin. Hence it is a subject of inquiry which can on no account be neglected. The art of war, then, is governed by five constant factors, to be taken into account in one's deliberations, when seeking to determine the conditions in the field. These are: (1) The Moral Law; (2) Heaven; (3) Earth; (4) The Commander; (5) Method and discipline [5].*

Are these definitions applicable to what is happening on the Internet today? Can these historical concepts be applied to the virtual world? Is the military perspective the right one to look at this problem with? The answer is a declarative YES—we felt this book was needed to help the national discussion on cyber. First there is no governing body to determine what definition we should use, so the definition is normally based on the perspective of the person speaking. Governments, finance companies, Internet providers, international corporations, organizations with a specific cause, and lawyers would all give us a different answer.

Tactical and Operational Reasons for Cyber War

The motivations are as old as time. Whether individuals or nations, it comes down to power or greed vs. defense of one's self or nation. Traditionally it was

> **NOTE**
>
> The tactical level of war is where individual battles are executed to achieve military objectives assigned to tactical units or task forces. In the Army this would normally be at the Brigade/Regimental level.
>
> The operational level of war is where multiple battles are combined into campaigns within a theater, or larger operational area. Activities at this level link strategy and tactics by establishing operational objectives needed to achieve the strategic objectives through a series of tactical battles. This would normally be at the Joint Task Force or Division level.
>
> The strategic level of war is where a nation, or coalition of nations, determines national political objectives that will be enforced by military forces and other instruments of national power. This is normally controlled at the Combatant Commander level and higher.

about controlling limited resources but today the power of a network is not determined by resources but the number of nodes on it which equates to the power of information/influence. Be it access to proprietary information, classified networks, interconnections on a social network, applications, data about customers, or systems that run the critical infrastructure, the more connected, the more value.

Today's critical infrastructure networks are key targets for cyber attack because they have grown to the point where they run the command and control systems, manage the logistics, enable the staff planning and operations and are the backbone of the intelligence capabilities. More importantly today, most command and control systems, as well as the weapon systems themselves, are connected to the Global Information Grid (GIG) or have embedded computer chips. Airplanes have become flying routers constantly receiving and sending targeting information. Air Defense and Artillery are guided by computers systems and they shoot smart munitions that adjust their flight based on Global Positioning System (GPS) updates to guide themselves to the target. The Intelligence Surveillance and Reconnaissance (ISR) systems gather so much information the challenge is sifting through it to find the critical data. Today's infantry squad has communication gear, GPS, tracking devices, cameras, and night vision devices. The computer chip is ubiquitous and has become one of the US centers of gravity. It is both our strength and could be turned into our weakness if taken away.

When we consider the military maxim "amateurs study tactics; professionals study logistics" [6],[1] it quickly becomes clear how important the logistical systems

---

[1]There is much dispute as to who uttered this military maxim. It has been attributed to General Omar Bradley and US Marine Corps Commandant General Robert H. Barrow. In various other forms, it has also been attributed to Napoleon, Helmuth von Moltke, and Carl von Clausewitz. For the purposes of this study, its origin is far less important than its message.

are. When we deploy forces into a theater of operations our capability to fight is shaped by the forces, weapons, equipment, and supplies that can be moved to the right place at the right time. Today, that is calculated and controlled by computers. An enemy can understand our intentions and abilities by tracking what is happening in the logistics system. If they can modify actions and data they can interdict, or at least impact, our capabilities.

Cyber Strategy and Power

There are some general principles we should look at when analyzing the virtual world. When deciding on military strategies we look to the Principles of War. When evaluating plans we evaluate Ends, Ways, and Means. When we analyze sources of national power we weigh, Diplomatic, Information, Military, and Economic (DIME) factors. Finally when we think of the national level tools we break them into hard power, soft power, and smart power. We will take a look at how all these apply to cyber warfare.

The US Principles of War are Objective, Offensive, Mass, Economy of Force, Maneuver, Unity of Command, Security, Surprise, and Simplicity [7]. As we look at cyber war we must decide if we are talking about the virtual battlefield of the Internet or the ubiquitous nature of cyber conflicts being enmeshed into the physical battlefield. Some of the principles don't easily transfer into the virtual battlefield but they all can be force multipliers in the physical battlefield. When deciding on a cyber strategy we must not throw out hundreds of years' worth of doctrine and tactics but rather understand how to modify it based on the new paradigm we are facing. This has been true of all the technical advancements on the battlefield that have caused a Revolution in Military Affairs (RMA). The key to success still lies in having a clear objective with a simple plan that utilizes surprise while protecting our infrastructure. The numerous news stories we see show that defending in cyber warfare is not easy, so offensive actions are still the best way to achieve victory (this is a military statement and ignores the legal/policy challenges that must be solved). Mass is still important to achieve impacts and is validated by botnets today. Economy of force and maneuver are more difficult to apply in a battlefield with attrition and terrain being relative terms.

When developing a strategic framework to determine how to defeat the enemy center of gravity it is important to validate the plan by analyzing ends, ways, and means. "Ends" is the objective, such as deny access to their command and control systems. "Ways" is the form through which a strategy is implemented, such as computer network attack or full scope Information Operations. "Means" consists of the resources available, such as people, equipment, and technology to execute the plan. We will look more closely at the "Means" when we analyze the sources of national power. So once we develop the plan that utilizes the Principles of War we use Ends/Ways/Means to validate whether we can execute it.

FIGURE 2.2 Instruments of National Power that Could Influence or be Influenced by Cyber Actions

When evaluating sources of national powers we analyze the Diplomatic, Information, Military, and Economic (DIME) factors seen in Figure 2.2. Diplomatic is based on the actions between states based on official communications. It can go through organizations like the State Department, National level Computer Emergency Response Teams (CERT), treaty organizations like NATO, economic groups like the Group of Twenty Finance Ministers and Central Bank Governors (G20), or law enforcement agencies. Next is Information, this power is based on controlling the key resource of the information age. It encompasses strategic communication, news and popular media, international opinion, social media sites, Open Source Intelligence (OSINT)—to include the collection, analysis, and dissemination on key national actors. Military is the final political option, but today we must understand this is full spectrum, from unconventional warfare, peacekeeping, humanitarian assistance, nation-building and finally large-scale combat operations. Economic power comes from the influence of trade, incentives like embargos and free trade zones and direct support like aid packages or sale of surplus DoD equipment. All these factors can be applied to effect behaviors in cyber warfare.

We will note that the concept of what constitutes instruments of national power is under review but the US Army's key counter insurgency doctrinal manual (FM 3-24) still uses DIME. Other acronyms are: MIDLIFE (Military, Intelligence, Diplomatic, Law Enforcement, Information, Finance, Economic), ASCOPE (Areas, Structures, Capabilities, Organizations, People, and Events) and PMESII (Political, Military, Economic, Social, Informational, Infrastructure) [8].

NOTE

The US military has six INTs that they use to manage intelligence collation. They are Open Source Intelligence (OSINT), Signals Intelligence (SIGINT), Imagery Intelligence (IMINT), Human Intelligence (HUMINT), Technical intelligence (TECHINT), and Measurement and Signature Intelligence (MASINT). The information from all these sources is fused into all-source analysis.

Cyber Arms Control

One idea that has become popular lately, related to cyber warfare, is the concept of arms control, or deterrence. The analogy is to the Cold War where everyone understood the concept of Nuclear War being impractical because it would cause Mutually Assured Destruction (MAD). There were just a few countries that could develop nukes so they worked together to avoid a war. The thought is that if we can make cyber attacks expensive, or the consequences so painful, nobody would use it. This worked because the cost of entry into the "Nuclear Capable" club was expensive and those in the club were all committed to not let anyone else in. Once both sides had the capability to kill the other side multiple times it lead to a series of incidents that convinced both sides it was a no win situation. Eventually a progression of international agreements reduced this threat. But MAD was an all or nothing scenario so is not a good fit for cyber warfare; let's look at another arms control agreement.

Another analogy is the international agreements on Biological Weapons. The issue is closer to cyber warfare in that it's easier to gain access to the weapons, if someone released a bio weapon it could impact the sender as much as the target, and once released it is impractical to control. The same problem exists with a computer virus released against a specific country, once someone reverse engineers it they can quickly send it back. The dangers were so intense that many countries agreed not to develop bio weapons. The challenge here was one of verification. It is impossible to track everyone who can develop these capabilities.

So generally when we talk about arms control it refers to Weapons of Mass Destruction (WMD), when we talk about cyber WMDs they are Weapons of Mass Disruption. There is no way to calculate the damage today. Rarely would a cyber attack result directly in deaths but could disrupt vital services that result in the damage to property, economic loss, or impacts to national security. This is not to say the potential is not there and we could see this becomes a method used by terrorists, but we are not seeing it today. The Cyber Policy Review stated that Industry estimates of losses from intellectual property to data theft in 2008 range as high as $1 trillion [9]. Most folks feel it is hard to justify raising cyber actions to the same level as systems that can cause mass causalities. The counter argument is there are so many critical infrastructure systems dependent on it that the unintended consequences of taking down major parts of the Internet could cause devastation at the national emergency level.

CYBER WAR—HYPE OR REALITY

The answer depends on the definition. To date no nation has declared a cyber war and although many governments have spoken out about cyber activities none have stated they suffered from an act of war. The two more talked about events are the 2007 cyber attacks against Estonia and the 2008 integrated cyber and kinetic attacks against Georgia. These both involve nation states and military action (Estonia called on NATO to send troops to help recover and Georgia had synchronized ground and cyber attacks). There are many other incidents most have been called criminal acts. This trend is very reminiscent to the US definition of "Terrorism." The US had a low level of terrorist acts because they were all listed as criminal acts, then after the Oklahoma bombing and 9/11 they updated the definition based on new priorities and the number of incidents shot up.

Some will say that the current state of affairs is just the *status quo*. To have the kind of growth the Internet has experienced it had to be net neutral and wide open. This resulted in many vulnerabilities being embedded into the system. Today so much is dependent on the Internet we want it to be safe and have declared it a national security issue. Folks who don't like the term cyber war feel there is a lot of hype spreading fear about the dangerous of a coming Cyber Pearl Harbor, or for the younger generation a Cyber 9/11, that is being used so the government can spend more on cyber protection and be used to erode our privacy rights.

In a recent debate *The Cyber War Threat Has Been Grossly Exaggerated* sponsored by Intelligence Squared US (IQ2US) hosted four well-know cyber experts to settle the matter. Marc Rotenberg and Bruce Schneier took the position that it was exaggerated and VADM (Ret) John M. (Mike) McConnell and Harvard Law Professor Jonathan Zittrain stated that we are in a cyber war. The results were: Pre-debate vote: For: 24% Against: 54% Undecided: 22%; Post-debate vote: For: 23% Against: 71% Undecided: 6%. The majority of the undecided shifted to a belief that the threat of a cyber war is real [10].

BOUNDARIES IN CYBER WARFARE

What do we mean by battlespace? The US military definition is: "A term used to signify a unified military strategy to integrate and combine armed forces for the military theatre of operations, including air, information, land, sea, and space to achieve military goals. It includes the environment, factors, and conditions that must be understood to successfully apply combat power, protect the force, or complete the mission. This includes enemy and friendly armed forces; infrastructure; weather; terrain; and the electromagnetic spectrum within the operational areas and areas of interest" [11]. In cyberspace, battlespace includes things such as the networks, computers, hardware (this includes weapon systems with embedded computer chips), software (commercial and government developed), applications (like command and control systems), protocols, mobile devices, and the people that run them.

Defense in Depth

Cybersecurity Defense in Depth is designed to build multiple layers of interconnected walls of protection around the network. It must be enhanced to protect against insider threats and mobile devices that migrate in and out of the perimeter but it is the standard practice for logical construction of a network. At the lowest level we have an individual home network behind our local Internet Service Provider (ISP) router, and at the other end of the spectrum we have a national state network like China behind their Great Firewall. The US government is behind a couple of hundred access points monitored by the Department of Homeland Security but then sub groups like Department of Defense, Department of Energy, Department of State, Department of Treasury (it is easy to see the trend) all sit behind their own security infrastructure. The amount of protection they deploy is based on their perception of risk and willingness to invest their profit back into security for the network. When we look at their defenses it is based on economic power rather than military power but they are at war nonetheless.

Computer Controlled Infrastructure

Next is the physical infrastructure, this includes—power, backup generators, Heating Ventilating and Air Conditioning (HVAC), surge control systems, connectivity (cabling), hardware, software, and people. The physical systems are vulnerable to surveillance, vandalism, sabotage, and attack. Much of this infrastructure is controlled by Industrial Control Systems (ICS) or as they are more commonly known Supervisory Control and Data Acquisition (SCADA) programs which are vulnerable to hacking or denial of service attacks. Note that SCADA is a subset of ICS but has become synonymous in the media. This list does not address the potential environmental disaster factors. If the threat cannot conduct a kinetic attack or hack the system then there is always the wetware vector. It is often easier to attack users than it is the equipment. So when attacking the physical there are a number of options to create the desired impact.

Organizational View

Organizations can be divided into commercial (including critical infrastructure) and government (generally divided into federal agencies and the military). These different organizations all approach cybersecurity differently. Most commercial companies are market driven and try to spend just enough on security to manage risk appropriately. These companies must make decisions based on Return on Investment (ROI) which leads to the eternal struggle between the Chief Financial Officer (CFO) and the Chief Information Officer (CIO). Today many CIOs calculate Return on

---

NOTE

US Critical Infrastructure includes: Agriculture and Food, Banking and Finance, Chemical, Commercial Facilities, Communications, Critical Manufacturing, Dams, Defense Industrial Base, Emergency Services, Energy, Government Facilities, Healthcare and Public Health, Information Technology, National Monuments and Icons, Nuclear Reactors, Materials and Waste, Postal and Shipping, Transportation Systems, and Water. Note that most of these are in private sector and government control which varies widely depending on the sector.

Security Investment using formulas like Annualized Loss Expectancy (Vulnerability × Threat × Asset Value = Total Risk then Total Risk × Countermeasures = Residual Risk). This would go something like: chance of getting a virus attack is 100%—in fact expect one a day, cost is 3 h of lost productivity and 1 h of IT support times total number of employees = 365 viruses × $450 labor × 200 people = $3,285,000 or buy antivirus for $40 per system for total of $8000 and reduce risk to acceptable level. With the need for cost saving in the government these types or calculations are becoming more common in the military today.

The DoD has a very hierarchical authority structure but it is not simple. Despite standing up CYBERCOM, the individual services (Army, Air Force, Navy/Marines) still have the authority and budget to decide how to implement cybersecurity. Each branch of the service has a name for their portion of the network. Defense Information Systems Agency (DISA) runs the Global Information Grid (GIG), Air Force has C2 Constellation, the Army has LandWarNet, and Navy has FORCEnet.

There are also different levels of classification on information and networks. The DoD uses Unclassified, For Official Use Only (FOUO), Secret, Top Secret, and Special Access Program/Special Access Required (SAP/SAR). The associated networks are Non-Secure Internet Protocol Router (NIPR) for unclassified, Secure Internet Protocol Router (SIPR) for secret, and Joint Worldwide Intelligence Communications System (JWICS) for Top Secret. In addition there are separate networks like the Defense Research and Engineering Network (DREN) for research. Finally, deployed forces build their own networks in theater that connect to many of these "reach back" networks as well as must connect to fellow coalition nations via multi-national forces networks. An example would be a unit from Fort Carson deployed to Afghanistan that would have to build a network in country or theater, would want to connect back to resources at Fort Carson, and connect to other international forces they are teamed with. It is not unusual to see a Tactical Operation Center (TOC) with 6–12 terminals representing the different networks. It is easy to see that there is not a clear chain of command for the network of networks supporting DoD.

As important as these networks are they don't include the full scope of the modern virtual battlefield. Today command and control of forces is done digitally, weapon systems are connected to the network and depend heavily on computing power, intelligence dominance is key to our ability to win on the modern battlefield and it is completely dependent on computer applications. During one military simulation a young Airman was asked what would happen if the network went down, he said they would have to stop flying. That is of course untrue as leaders of the pre-digital generation were flying similar missions long before computers were used for command and control but the generation perception and dependence on the network was startling. Note that the loss of the TOC network would have a huge impact on the ability to process orders nearly as fast or accurately as the current "information dominance" systems allow.

When we talk about CYBERCOM and the Services (Army, Navy, Air Force) it is important to remember that the Services train and equip the forces and the Combatant Commanders call on the services to provide forces for their missions. Strategic

Command (STRATCOM) has the mission to "ensure US freedom of action in space and cyberspace" [12]. Next is Cyber Command (CYBERCOM) whose mission is to "plan, coordinate, integrate, synchronize, and conduct activities to: direct the operations and defense of specified Department of Defense information networks and, prepare to, and when directed, conduct full-spectrum military cyberspace operations in order to enable actions in all domains, ensure US/Allied freedom of action in cyberspace and deny the same to our adversaries" [12]. Each Service has a Cyber unit that supports CYBERCOM, the Air Force has the "24th Number Air Force," the Army has "Army Cyber," the Navy has the "10th Fleet" and the Marines have "Marine Forces Cyber." Closely aligned to these forces is the Intelligence Community—specifically the National Security Agency (NSA). This results in different priorities based on the different mission each organization has.

It is important to note that there are US Codes that set the rules for how these units operate. There are a number of titles that provide specific guidance. Title 10 is Armed Forces and is the law that regulates how war is fought [11]. Title 50 is War and National Defense and generally covers intelligence and counter intelligence [11]. It is interesting to note that some units had their authorized mission changed from being under Title 50 to Title 10 as part of the CYBERCOM stand up. Title 18 is Crimes and Criminal Procedure which covers taking the attacking party to court [11]. Many people are now talking about the need to integrate these three into one integrated process (sometimes called Title 78). Other titles that often used are Title 32 which is National Guard and Title 14 which is the Coast Guard [11]. These forces are not as restricted by laws like Posse Comitatus which restricts the federal government use of the military for law enforcement. Today we see Joint Operation Centers with forces from multiple "title sources" or "forces" to allow them to operate effectively based on the different rules they must comply with.

WHERE CYBER FITS IN THE WAR-FIGHTING DOMAINS

Historically there were only two war-fighting domains, land and sea. Land is simply the area where combatants fought. Over time there were developments in weapons that would give one side or the other an advantage but they would face each other on the field-of-battle. Then the sea became both a separate war-fighting domain and a part of the land domain. The Maritime domain [13] includes the oceans, seas, bays, estuaries, islands, coastal areas, and the airspace above these, including the littorals. The littorals have two operational environments: Seaward, the area from the open ocean to the shore, which must be controlled to support operations ashore and Landward, the area inland from the shore that can be supported and defended directly from the sea. Ships would fight battles to both control the sea and support land battles. As technology continued to influence the battlefield, airplanes were introduced. The air domain is the atmosphere, beginning at the Earth's surface and extending to the altitude where its effects upon operations become negligible [13]. The first airplanes were used for reconnaissance but were soon armed and fought both air to air and air to ground engagements. Then warfare reached space. Space is the environment corresponding to the space domain, where electromagnetic radiation, charged particles, and electric and magnetic fields are the dominant physical influences, and that encompasses the earth's ionosphere and magnetosphere, interplanetary space, and the solar atmosphere [14]. This was a unique domain as it was used by the other domains rather than a domain where combat was fought (though at some point it will become another battlefront). Finally cyberspace became so vital to the war-fighters it was declared a domain. It is a global domain within the information environment consisting of the interdependent network of information technology infrastructures, including the Internet, telecommunications networks, computer systems, and embedded processors and controllers [14]. Modern commanders depend on it and are actively studying how to fight and win the next war on it.

Land

As we look back at the progression of warfare on land we see there have been many Revolutions of Military Affairs (RMA). The rock gave way to the club, which was beat out by the spear and then the bow. Horse-mounted soldiers had an advantage over ground troops and then the stirrup gave them a tremendous advantage. Guns and artillery increased the rate at which armies could kill each other as well as the effective range at which they could kill. Then came the tank and machinegun. Each of these RMA changed how armies fought. New doctrine, tactics, and organizational structures had to be developed. Should we integrate the new weapons into every unit or build a unit of pure machineguns/tanks? The decision was tank units should consist on tanks by themselves but the machinegun should be integrated into every unit. The decision to make tank units of pure tanks has been reversed. Today, the tank is normally integrated with infantry to form "combined arms task forces" so the commander can leverage each unit's strengths. These historical lessons in transformation must be studied to find how to most efficiently develop methods of fighting in cyberspace.

Sea

In many ways the sea is an analogous battlefield to cyberspace. Like cyberspace it is a large area where ships can easily move without detection so the defender has the challenge of detecting where the threat is. No one side can control it. The criminal elements operating on the Internet are comparable to the pirates of old who would interdict and influence the lines of commerce. There were eventually international agreements developed to deal with these threats. Another example we can draw from the Navy is the development of the Flattop or Aircraft Carrier. For years the battleship was the measure of a nation's sea power but the introduction of the Flattop caused a paradigm shift and soon strategies, doctrine, and tactics were built around it. Most senior officers had built their careers around the battleship and the defense industrial base was heavily investing in the battleship so they strongly resisted the transformation. They refused to see the need to change based on a new capability. This cultural blindness is impacting the transformation to computer network operations in many of today's organizations. At the tactical level many security professionals still base their strategies on outdated technologies, even though the industry and the battlespace have transformed, and evolved. They are still focused on perimeter defenses and ignore the mobile devices being used by their work force. At the senior leadership level the lack of understanding of the technology and its implications in some organizations are impeding the development of doctrine to fight the next war.

Air

Airpower is similar to cyber power because it is a domain dominated by technological advancements. Early on there were major leaders developing strategies, doctrine, and tactics. General Giulio Douhet was an Italian officer who was one of the first real theorists supporting the use of Air Power [15]. He felt that there was no defense against bombers, it would terrorize populations into surrender, and he advocated the use of explosive, incendiary, and poison gas bombs against population centers as everyone contributes to the total war effort so everyone is legitimate target. General Douhet was court-martialed for his outspoken beliefs.

Space

Space is very comparable to cyberspace in that it is generally considered to be an enabler to the other domains. It provides communications paths for most long haul communications systems, Command and Control (C2), Intelligence Surveillance and Reconnaissance (ISR), navigation based on Global Positioning System (GPS), phones-radios-television-financial transactions, and surveillance for wide area reconnaissance-weather-mapping and commercial imaging (i.e. Google maps). The George C. Marshall Institute produced a great series called "A Day without Space" which lays out all the impacts. Space provides some great examples on how to integrate a new technology into the armed forces. Space started as a military dominated domain that has transitioned to a commercial market just like cyber operations. It is a technology that integrated into the other domains to the point they are dependent on it. It is an area that requires unique skills so the management of the work force presents a challenge. It takes time to build senior leaders for a new technology and as the commercial demand takes off the competition for the workforce gets fierce. It is very hard to retain skilled operators in cyberspace related fields.

Cyber Domain

Cyber is ubiquitous in all the other modern domains. "I think that a day without cyber brings you back to about World War I days," said Lt. Gen. William T. Lord, Air Force chief of war-fighting information [16]. When we talk about the cyber domain some will say it is limited to the hardware that runs the military networks (computers, routers, firewalls), others will say it is the military networks and the supporting infrastructure (i.e. defense contractors and long haul communications providers), a few believe it is all government systems, still others feel it is all systems connected to the Internet (all private and governments systems). As we look for precedents we can see Maritime law could be used, or international space treaties could apply or maybe we could develop a cyber manifest destiny. Some of the answers are overly simple or fit within current legal rules but ignore the reality of how interconnected these systems are. The problem is complex and, much like defining the boundaries in an insurgency conflict, may require different answers for different audiences. This domain is in need of theorists, strategies, doctrine, and tactics that shape what the domain and cyber war itself is scoped to include and exclude.

SUMMARY

We studied the traditional war-fighting domains of land, sea, air, and space both as they relate to cyber operations and what we can learn from them as we develop cyber as a war-fighting domain. Many US citizens would say the last time the country was at war was World War II. Others would say Korea and Vietnam were wars but the counter is that technically they were police actions. If Korea was a war then we are still at war with North Korea [having stood on the Demilitarized Zone (DMZ) between the two countries most soldiers would agree]. Many presidents have openly talked about the Cold War but a "war" was never declared. The US declared a "War on Drugs" and "War on Terrorism" but again it was not a war against another country but rather on a problem that had reached the level it was a national security issue, if this is the standard we measure by then we could have a pure cyber war. The US has been in multiple wars in the Middle East (Iraq twice and Afghanistan) but these were not formally declared "wars," some would say they are part of the "War on Terrorism." Still others will talk about economic warfare. The last time America was in a formal war was World War II, the concept of what a war means is changing. These have been very traditional wars and if they are the standards we measure a "war" by then there is no such thing as cyber war.

Today the Internet is very similar to how the Wild West is portrayed in movies. Over the course of a movie they might have to deal with Indian attacks, Mexican banditos, bad weather, criminals from our own community and Mexican Army invasions. Indian attacks are a form of guerilla warfare, banditos are non-state actors but may have informal support from their host nation, weather equates to the environmental impacts that create noise in the system making things unpredictable, criminal acts if they get bad enough may become a threat to the community and may require the aid of the state or federal government to solve and military invasion is a full scope war which could require the full weight of the country to address. Any of these can wipe us out and may need to be addressed by the local sheriff, the rangers or the US Army depending on how the politicians choose to react. So the question of if we are in a cyber war today is answered by the simple statement "don't care what we call it just get us some help!"

REFERENCES

[1] Defense, Secretary of DoD Publications [online]. <http://www.dtic.mil/doctrine/new_pubs/jp3_13.pdf>.

[2] Defense, Secretary of DoD Publications [online]. <http://www.dod.mil/pubs/foi/joint_staff/jointStaff_jointOperations/07-F-2105doc1.pdf>.

[3] Nations, United. UN terms [online, cited August 17, 2010]. <http://unterm.un.org/dgaacs/unterm.nsf/375b4cb457d6e2cc85256b260070ed33/$searchForm?SearchView>.

[4] Bassford C. The Clausewitz homepage. On war [document on the Internet, cited August 30, 2010]. <http://www.clausewitz.com/readings/OnWar1873/TOC.htm>.

[5] Sun Tzu on the art of war [document on the Internet, cited August 17, 2010]. <http://www.chinapage.com/sunzi-e.html>.

[6] Wright Donald P, Reese Colonel Timothy R. On Point II: transition to the new campaign the United States Army in Operation Iraqi Freedom May 2003–January 2005. Part IV: Sustaining the campaign Chapter 12 logistics and combat service support operations [online, cited August 21, 2010]. <http://www.globalsecurity.org/military/library/report/2008/onpoint/chap12.htm>.

[7] Joint Doctrine Division, J-7, Joint Staff. DOD Dictionary of Military and Associated Terms [document on the Internet, cited August 30, 2010]. <http://www.dtic.mil/doctrine/dod_dictionary/index.html>.

[8] Kem Colonel (Retired) Jack D. Understanding the operational environment: the expansion of DIME [online, cited August 21, 2010]. <http://www.thefreelibrary.com/Understanding+the+operational+environment%3A+the+expansion+of+DIME.-a0213693824>.

[9] Securing our digital future. The White House blog. Washington, DC [document on the Internet, cited August 17, 2010]. <http://www.whitehouse.gov/CyberReview/>.

[10] IQ2US, Intelligence Squared US Debate – "The cyber war threat has been grossly exaggerated." Washington DC, USA: s.n.; June 8, 2010. <http://intelligencesquaredus.org/index.php/past-debates/cyber-war-threat-has-been-grossly-exaggerated/>.

[11] Congress. US House [online, cited September 7, 2010]. <http://uscode.house.gov/>.

[12] DoD. STRATCOM. Strategic command [online, cited September 7, 2010]. <http://www.stratcom.mil/>.

[13] DoD. Joint Electronic Library [online, cited September 7, 2010]. <http://www.dtic.mil/doctrine/>.

[14] Dictionary of Military and associated terms. DoD [online, cited August 30, 2010]. <http://www.dtic.mil/doctrine/dod_dictionary/index.html>.

[15] Air force historical studies page. Out of print [online, cited: September 7, 2010]. <http://www.airforcehistory.hq.af.mil/Publications/fulltext/command_of_the_air.pdf>.

[16] Grant Rebecca. Battling the Phantom menace. airforce-magazine.com [online]. <http://www.airforce-magazine.com/MagazineArchive/Pages/2010/April%202010/0410menace.aspx>.

REFERENCES

Cyber Doctrine

INFORMATION IN THIS CHAPTER:

- Current US Doctrine
- Sample Doctrine / Strategy From Around the World
- Some Key Military Principles that Must be Adapted to Cyber Warfare

Doctrine is the fundamental principle by which the military forces or elements thereof guide their actions in support of national objectives. It is authoritative but requires judgment in application [1]. It is what militaries based their plans on. It is influenced by tradition, and guides Tactics Techniques and Procedures (TTPs). We will cover what doctrine exists today, what doctrine needs to be translated to cyberspace, what adjacent guidance exists in non-military agencies and, finally, what exercises are being conducted to develop doctrine.

CURRENT US DOCTRINE

The United States Military does not have a definition for cyber warfare today. Over time this capability has been called computer security, Information Security (InfoSec), Net Centric Warfare, Information Assurance (IA), Information Warfare, Cybersecurity, and now Cyber Warfare. These terms generally focused on the defense, today when military planners use the term cyber they include offensive capabilities as well. Cyber is generally understood to be Computer Network Operations (CNO). There are three functions under CNO: Computer Network Exploitation (CNE), Computer Network Attack (CNA), and Computer Network Defense (CND). These functions map to traditional doctrinal terms: CNE is not what programmers think of for exploitation but is more like reconnaissance or espionage and will be covered in chapter 5, CNA is offense and is also covered in chapter 5 and CND is defensive operations which is examined in chapter 7.

CNO falls under Information Operations (IO) which has a set of core, supporting, and related capabilities—see Figure 3.1 for details. There are two areas that overlap—CNO and Information Assurance (IA). CNO is defined by the three functions listed above while IA is defined as measures that protect and defend

Information Operations (IO)

Core Capabilities

• Psychological Operation

• Military Deception

• Operations Security

      o *Computer Network Operations*

           ▪ *Computer Network Attack*

           ▪ *Computer Network Defense*

           ▪ *Computer Network Exploitati(*

• Electronic Warfare

• Electronic Attack

• Electronic Protection

• Electronic Support

Supporting Capabilities

• *Information Assurance*

• Physical Security

• Combat Camera

• Counterintelligence

• Physical Attack

Related Capabilities

• Public Affairs

• Civil-Military Operations

• Defense Support to Public Diplomacy

FIGURE 3.1 Information Operations Framework [1]

information and information systems by ensuring their availability, integrity, authentication, confidentiality, and non-repudiation. This includes providing for restoration of information systems by incorporating protection, detection, and reaction capabilities [1]. So we can think of IA as building and maintaining the networks while CNO is planning and conducting battle over them, much like the difference between maintaining the Tanks in an Armor Battalion and using them to fight a battle.

There are some concerns with how cyber doctrine is being developed today. The key Joint Publication for cyber doctrine (JP 3-13) was published in 2006. Doctrine is not normally updated quickly, so when we have the environment operating under Moore's Law (capabilities doubling every 18 months) there is concern that the doctrine will quickly become out of date. Another potential issue is that the services donot follow the same terminology; the Army and the Air Force have different definitions of Information Operations. Then there is the challenge of having much of the doctrine classified, this leads to different groups having access to different information and basing decisions on only the information they have access to. Finally there is the problem with basic attitude on the importance of cyber warfare as part of combat operations with some leaders belief that cyberspace is only a supporting function for administrative activities while others feel cyberspace is embedded in everything from today's command and control systems to the weapons systems and it is the critical center of gravity for the nation (often this division runs along the lines of techies and luddites).

US Forces

The White House released its International Strategy for Cyberspace in May 2011 with focus on prosperity, security, and openness in a networked world. "The United States will pursue an international cyberspace policy that empowers the innovation that drives our economy and improves lives here and abroad. In all this work, we are grounded in principles essential not just to American foreign policy, but to the future of the Internet itself. Focus on freedom of information and privacy" [2]. It had an overall goal with key objectives:

- Goal = the United States will work internationally to promote an open, interoperable, secure, and reliable information and communications infrastructure that supports international trade and commerce, strengthens international security, and fosters free expression and innovation. To achieve that goal, we will build and sustain an environment in which norms of responsible behavior guide states' actions, sustain partnerships, and support the rule of law in cyberspace.
- Diplomatic Objective = the United States will work to create incentives for, and build consensus around an international environment in which states— recognizing the intrinsic value of an open, interoperable, secure, and reliable cyberspace—work together and act as responsible stakeholders.
- Defense Objective = the United States will, along with other nations, encourage responsible behavior and oppose those who would seek to disrupt networks and systems, dissuading and deterring malicious actors, and reserving the right to defend these vital national assets as necessary and appropriate.

Department of Defense Strategy for Operating in Cyberspace was released in July 2011 and has fire initiatives:

- Strategic Initiative 1: Treat cyberspace as an operational domain to organize, train, and equip so that DoD can take full advantage of cyberspace's potential.
- Strategic Initiative 2: Employ new defense operating concepts to protect DoD networks and systems.
- Strategic Initiative 3: Partner with other US government departments and agencies and the private sector to enable a whole-of-government cybersecurity strategy.

- Strategic Initiative 4: Build robust relationships with US allies and international partners to strengthen collective cybersecurity.
- Strategic Initiative 5: Leverage the nation's ingenuity through an exceptional cyber workforce and rapid technological innovation.

US CYBERCOM has been given responsibility for cyberspace operations. In a memo signed on 23 June 2009 the US Secretary of Defense established the new command [3]. Gen. Keith Alexander is its first Commander and in the recent statement to congress said, "The Department of Defense networks that we defend are probed roughly 250,000 times an hour" [3]. By 2006, to cite another example, the Department determined that 10–20 terabytes of data had been remotely exfiltrated from NIPRNet [3]. He then quoted Deputy Secretary William Lynn who recently noted that the key to Cyber Command is its "linking of intelligence, offense, and defense under one roof" [3]. The National Security Agency (NSA) contributes essential expertise to accomplish this. Gen. Alexander stated "US Cyber Command has three main lines of operation. We direct the operations and defense of the Global Information Grid so the Department of Defense can perform its missions, we stand ready to execute full-spectrum cyber operations on command, and we stay prepared to defend our nation's freedom of action in cyberspace" [3]. Cyber Command will use five principles for the Department's strategy in cyberspace: Remember that cyberspace is a defensible domain, Make our defenses active, Extend protection to our critical infrastructure, Foster collective defenses, and Leverage US technological advantages [4]. This focus on bringing cyber doctrine and policy to the highest level of command in the military shows how much emphasis the leadership is placing on this new warfighting domain. There is not a lot of money to make this happen until the new command catches up with the DoD Program Objective Memorandum (POM) budgeting cycle so they have had to reallocate funds, but they are making it happen now because they feel it is vital to the future success of the military. Figure 3.2 shows the large number of cyber centers that need to be coordinated across the US government. Many believe CyberCom is best positioned to accomplish this mission but doctrinally that responsibility lies with Department of Homeland Security.

While this command has been stood up the The Honorable W. "Mac" Thornberry Chairman of Subcommittee on Emerging Threats and Capabilities Committee on Armed Services House of Representatives has called out the fact "DOD does not yet have an overarching budget estimate for full-spectrum cyberspace operations including computer network attack, computer network exploitation, and classified funding. During February and March 2011, DOD provided Congress with three different views of its cybersecurity budget estimates for fiscal year 2012 ($2.3 billion, $2.8 billion, and $3.2 billion, respectively) that included different elements of DOD's cybersecurity efforts [3]. The three budget views are largely related to the Defense-wide Information Assurance Program and do not include all full-spectrum cyber operation costs, such as computer network exploitation and computer network attack, which are funded through classified programs from the national intelligence and military intelligence program budgets" [5].

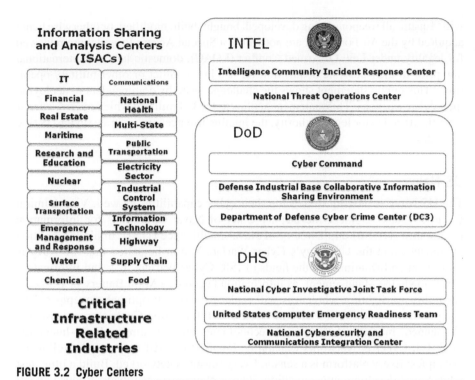

FIGURE 3.2 Cyber Centers

The key to understanding where the authority controlling cybersecurity is the same as any other function of the government, follow the money. A new command or presidential directive without funding is more posturing than executing a plan of action. Naming someone into a new position or declaring a new committee that doesnot have budget authority is more public relations than fixing a problem. When we look at a lot of the activity it is key to see who controls the resources.

US Air Force

The initial US Air Force commander of 24th AF Major General Richard E. Webber told congress his number one priority for 24th AF is developing and improving cyberspace situational awareness. They have also established a Cyber Operations Liaison Element (COLE) to act as liaison officers (LNO) to facilitate the requisite exchange of expertise between mission planners and Cyber planners [6]. The Air Force has made the greatest efforts to establish cyber operations integration into their forces today. They were the first to move to stand up a cyber command, and have aggressively tried to take the lessons learned from developing doctrine and organizational structure for space and apply it to cyberspace.

The Air Force also published Air Force Instruction 51-402 July 27, 2011 Legal Reviews of weapons and cyber capabilities which states the Judge Advocate General will "Ensure all weapons being developed, bought, built, modified, or otherwise being acquired by the Air Force that are not within a Special Access Program are reviewed for legality under Law Of Armed Conflict (LOAC), domestic law and international law prior to their possible acquisition for use in a conflict or other military operation." This public statement shows the challenge faced by commanders in deploying their cyber weapons. This statement applies to the US military which operates under US title 10 codes for legal authority, the intelligence agencies operate under US title 50 codes.

US Navy

The US Navy is moving to develop their cyber capabilities as well. Vice Admiral David J. "Jack" Dorsett, the Deputy Chief of Naval Operations for Information Dominance (N2/N6) and Director of Naval Intelligence (DNI), in his Information Dominance and the US Navy's Cyber Warfare Vision he stated that the Navy is Prominent and Dominant in the fields of ISR, Cyber Warfare, C2, and Information and Knowledge Management, as information becomes a Main Battery of US Navy capability warfighting wholeness will replace today sub-optimal stovepipes. The Navy will move to From Platform-Centric to Information-Centric processes, Into Unmanned, machine Autonomous technologies and Creating a Fully-Integrated Intel, C2, Cyber & Networks Capability. Finally they will focus on the following principles: Every platform is a sensor, Every sensor is networked, Build a little; test a lot, Spiral development/acquisition, Plug-n-play sensor payloads, Reduce afloat/ airborne manning, Transition to remoted, automated, One operator controls multiple platforms, and Emphasize UAS and autonomous platforms [7]. This list of goals is based on the Navies desire to deploy capabilities faster and cheaper. The Navy looked to its history and wanted to take lessoned learned from standing up the 10th fleet during World War II to deal with the new submarine threat and apply that same methodology of innovation and focus on how new technology is impacting the battlespace. They have made some hard choices like reorganizing the staff functions to increase efficiencies and integration by joining the N2 (Intelligence) and N6 (Communications/Networks) functions into the Information Dominance directorate. These changes show the level of importance and time sensitivity is placing on the potential for cyber warfare, they do not want to be caught preparing to fight the last war.

US Army

The US Army is formally addressing cyber doctrine development today. The US Army Training and Doctrine Command (TRADOC) has coordinated concept development for cyber warfare with stakeholders across the Army, and in January of this year published a Cyberspace Operations (CO) Concept Capabilities Plan (CCP) which outlines the framework under which the Army expects to conduct cyber operations in the timeframe 2016–2028. They are focusing on three dimensions of cyber in the current operational environment: psychological contest of wills, strategic engagement, and the cyber-electromagnetic contest. CyberOps encompass those actions to gain the advantage, protect that advantage, and place adversaries at a disadvantage in the cyber-electromagnetic contest. CyberOps are not an end to themselves, but rather an integral part of Fire Support Operations and include activities prevalent in peacetime military engagement, which focus on winning the cyber-electromagnetic contest. CyberOps are continuous; engagements occur daily, most often without the commitment of additional forces. Consequently, the framework developed for Army Operations establishes four components for CyberOps: cyber warfare (CyberWar), cyber network operations (CyNetOps), cyber support (CyberSpt), and cyber situational awareness (CyberSA) see Figure 3.3 for how they interrelate [8]. The Army is the one service that likes to write doctrine, they want to have it taught in their school houses (at every level) as a way to push new doctrine into the field. This is a different approach from the other services that are focused on reorganization; the Army wants to reeducate their force to understand the new environment.

The Army is moving out of the classroom as well. The Army wants the ability to fight in Cyberspace and to deploy a new arsenal of cyber warfare weapons. Lt. Gen. Rhett Hernandez, the commander of Army Cyber Command/Second Army, said the plan is to acquire both defensive and offensive capabilities—including tools to conduct network damage assessments and ensure that there is no collateral harm done to non-military entities. Commanders in the field should have a "full range of cyberspace capabilities" at their hands including the ability to "seize, retain, and exploit" enemy networks, he said November 8 at the Milcom conference in Baltimore, Md. The Army "seeks the same level of freedom to operate in cyberspace

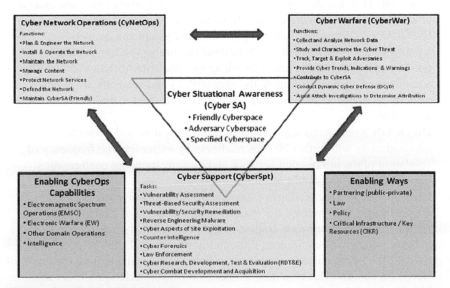

FIGURE 3.3 CyNetOps Framework [8]

domain as we have in the land domain," he said. The command, which became operational in October 2010, is in its infancy [9]. The US Army's first-of-its-kind dedicated computer network security brigade is now operational and has been deployed in support of combat-active units in the field. The 780th Military Intelligence Brigade, originally conceived in 2008, will be utilized in a limited capacity until the teams are fully operational in 2015. "We have an expeditionary cyber capability to assist Army units in defense of their networks. We have a team that is forward deployed right now in Afghanistan. They go forward to help the brigade combat team secure their networks," said the brigade's commander, Col. John Sweet [10]. These organizational changes inside the typical planning cycle show the dedication senior military leaders have to moving at the speed of need to build and deploy cyber warfare capabilities.

DoD INFOCONs

The last thing we will cover in current US military doctrine is Information Operations Condition (INFOCON) system procedures [11]. This is the guidance for all DoD systems to direct the state of the defensive posture the military networks must take when under attack. The INFOCON increases from 5 to 1 when under more severe attacks.

- INFOCON 5 (normal activity). This is the normal state of readiness of information systems and networks (i.e. "Routine" Network Operations (NetOps)) that can be sustained indefinitely. System and network administrators will create and maintain a snapshot of each server and workstation in a normal operational condition. This snapshot then becomes the normal operational baseline that can be compared against future changes to identify unauthorized activities.
- INFOCON 4 (increased vigilance procedures). System and network administrators will establish an operational rhythm to validate the known good image of an information network against the current state and identify unauthorized changes. Additionally, user profiles and accounts are reviewed and checks are conducted for dormant accounts. Impact to end-users should be negligible.
- INFOCON 3 (enhanced readiness procedures). System and network administrators will further NetOps readiness by increasing the frequency of validation of the information network and its corresponding configuration. Impact to end-users should be minor.
- INFOCON 2 (greater readiness procedures). System and network administrators will increase the frequency of validation of NetOps readiness for the information network. Impact to end-users could be significant for short periods, which can be mitigated through training and scheduling.
- INFOCON 1 (maximum readiness procedures). This is the highest condition of NetOps readiness. This condition addresses intrusion techniques that cannot be identified or defeated at lower readiness levels. During INFOCON 1, System

> **WARNING**
>
> When dealing with an attack or intrusion, the normal response is to recover systems as soon as possible. This will often destroy evidence necessary to determine how the systems were compromised in the first place. If we don't do the forensic work before the reload, it will be impossible to figure out what we need to fix to prevent the threat from coming right back. The key is to ensure we have a process to preserve the evidence offline while the systems are recovered.

and Network Administrators may reload the operating system software on key infrastructure servers from an accurate baseline. Once baseline comparisons no longer indicate anomalous activities, INFOCON 1 would be terminated. Impact to end-users could be significant for short periods, which can be mitigated through training and scheduling.

- Tailored Readiness Options (TROs). TROs are supplemental measures to respond to specific intrusion characteristics. They are narrowly focused and meant to supplement the current INFOCON readiness level. TROs will document, in standard language, all supplemental INFOCON measures to ensure a common understanding of the level of readiness and mission impact of each measure.

There are some issues: these INFOCONs are not regularly exercised and there is some doubt as to the viability of the current IT staffs to be able to execute this intensive schedule. The good news is these are much better reaction guidelines than the old set which lead to organizations disconnecting themselves during an attack causing a self-denial of service. Any local commander can increase the level of INFOCON but may not lower the level of protection below the next higher command. Finally a TRO is a unique reaction to a specific threat; the most recent example is the reaction to malware on thumb drives. DoD disallowed the use of thumb drives deciding that the operational impact of losing the capability was less that the threat of compromising their network.

SAMPLE DOCTRINE / STRATEGY FROM AROUND THE WORLD

We will now review some of the cyber doctrine and strategies being developed by other nations. We will start with China and some of the other major Asian countries. Then cover European countries. While Russia is a major player most of their impact is in crime vs warfare so will not call them out uniquely. Finally, we will look at possibility of private or mercenary organizations.

Chinese Doctrine

The next nation we will look at is China. As early as 1999 China was developing doctrine on how to compensate for military technological inferiority against the United States. Some of their senior strategists published a document called

"Unrestricted Warfare." It was insightful that they were thinking about the value of network warfare already, but statements like, "Technology is like 'magic shoes' on the feet of mankind, and after the spring has been wound tightly by commercial interests, people can only dance along with the shoes, whirling rapidly in time to the beat that they set," [12] shows how differently a culture can shape how doctrine is developed.

Taiwan watches Chinese strategies very closely, and published a good analytical review of new doctrine being considered by the People's Liberation Army (PLA) [13]. The following is a list of the more pertinent concepts:

- Highly controlled war is a new form of warfare in which "the direct purpose is to control a political regime, and in which political, economic, diplomatic, and other resources are integrated effectively to control the scale, form, means, and results of the war, with the backing of absolute military superiority."
- Acupuncture war, which establishes the examination of critical points in a network that, much like the pressure points in martial arts, when taken out, can shut down an entire system. In acupuncture war using Electronic Warfare (EW) can enable "the first battle being the final battle."
- Strategic information war, which is understood to be the integration of political, economic, military, diplomatic, and other areas to produce an overall or comprehensive information victory. The targets of strategic Information Warfare (IW) include national political, monetary, communications, and other crucial sectors down to single weapon systems such as aircraft carriers.
- Work Web sites, which have established distant learning capabilities and databases for quick access to information not readily available in the past.
- Intangible war, which focuses on strategies, market competition, legal systems, and intellectual property rights. These are areas of importance that the West must not overlook.
- Net Force is a brand new type of 'Grand War' scheme that combines high-tech knowledge with politics, economy, psychology, and information networks and that is 'all people being soldiers, the integration of peace and warfare, and dual usage for the military and civilians.'
- Surgical warfare aims to attack the vulnerability of high-tech weapons systems to achieve final victory, namely, attacking one point to cripple the whole system.
- Space warfare capability puts the crowning touch on China's asymmetric warfare capability: the ability to sabotage or destroy an enemy's space systems.

The "US-China Economic and Security Review Commission Report on the Capability of the People's Republic of China to Conduct Cyber Warfare and Computer Network Exploitation." It states "The government of the People's Republic of China (PRC) is a decade into a sweeping military modernization program that has fundamentally transformed its ability to fight high-tech wars. The Chinese military, using increasingly networked forces capable of communicating across service arms and among all echelons of command, is pushing beyond its traditional missions focused on Taiwan and toward a more regional defense posture. This modernization effort, known as informationization, is guided by the doctrine of fighting "Local War Under Informationized Conditions," which refers to the PLA's ongoing effort to develop a fully networked architecture capable of coordinating military operations on land, in air, at sea, in space and across the electromagnetic spectrum [14]. "This open source study reveals how seriously China is modernizing their Cyber Forces for today's ongoing cyber war and the next integrated kinetic/non-kinetic war.

The Annual Report to Congress Military and Security Developments Involving the People's Republic of China 2011 states that China's developing capabilities for cyber warfare is consistent with authoritative PLA military writings. Two military doctrinal writings, Science of Strategy and Science of Campaigns identify information warfare (IW) as integral to achieving information superiority and an effective means for countering a stronger foe. Although neither document identifies the specific criteria for employing computer network attack against an adversary, both advocate developing capabilities to compete in this medium.

In a separate report it was pointed out that as few as 12 different Chinese groups, largely backed or directed by the government there, do the bulk of the China-based cyberattacks stealing critical data from US companies and government agencies, according to US cybersecurity analysts and experts. The aggressive, but stealthy attacks, which steal billions of dollars in intellectual property and data, often carry distinct signatures allowing US officials to link them to certain hacker teams. And, analysts say the US often gives the attackers unique names or numbers, and at times can tell where the hackers are and even who they may be [15]. This targeting can result in accusations and political posturing but to date no military action has been authorized. Much like the Cold War it is more about gathering information but unlike the Cold War were military capabilities were displayed as part of a show of force but not used many of the cyber weapons are being actively used.

Finally from Wikileaks documents, and several other sources, the identity and location of the main Chinese Cyber War operation is now known. The Chinese Chengdu Province First Technical Reconnaissance Bureau (1st TRB) is a Chinese Army electronic warfare unit located in central China (Chengdu), and is the most frequent source of hacking attacks traced back to their source. The servers used by the 1st TRB came online over five years ago, and are still used. The Chinese government flatly refuses to even discuss the growing pile of evidence regarding operations like the 1st TRB [16]. So we can see China is using both civilian hackers and military Computer Network Attack units to engage in cyber operations.

TIP

The information being posted to Wikileaks has changed the paradigm of insider threats. Both commercial and government organizations are now relooking internal trust. With hackers breaking in and posting information to Wikileaks and insiders handing over large amounts of data that reporters can poor through it is time for senior leaders to reevaluate their insider protections and risk acceptance.

What does all this focus on modernization and cyber doctrine mean? The level of effort and types of activities mentioned above show that China is preparing to fight the next war utilizing the electromagnetic spectrum and plan to deign access to their enemy. They understand how dependant the West has become on the IT infrastructure, and will attack that center of gravity. They are conducting reconnaissance today that will give them the advantage. They have the infrastructure to conduct denial of service attacks. They have talked about attacking the integrity of systems so their enemy cannot trust their command and control systems to give accurate reports. China is not alone in this level of cyber warfare doctrinal development but they are in the front of the pack.

Other Asian countries

Japan has placed their strategy under the Japanese Ministry of Defense (MoD) Self-Defense Forces National Information Security Center (NISC). In 2005, NISC was established following a surge in cyber attacks. The government-wide agency was set up to co-ordinate efforts to protect computer networks. In February 2009, the Japanese government adopted the Second National Strategy on Information Security (NSIS) for the years 2009–2011. The 3-year plan includes four subjects: central and local governments, critical infrastructure, business entities, and individuals. As part of the NSIS process, the Japanese government adopted "Secure Japan 2009." One-fourth of its 212 policy items are aimed at the improvement of central and local governments. In the areas devoted to critical infrastructure and business entities, private enterprises serve as the subjects of its actions while the government provides support [17]. Japan is developing cyber doctrine with a broader government focus, they want to ensure the country is secure from attacks, and are willing to leverage their military capabilities to achieve it.

South Korea vs North Korea: South Korea's Defense Security Command (DSC) and the Ministry of National Defense (MND) stated in December 2009 that hackers had accessed classified military plans drawn up by South Korea and the US. Details of "Operation Plan 5027," which outlines how South Korea would be defended in the event of war, were said to have been transferred to an internet protocol (IP) address in China but thought to be compromised. The reaction was to stand up a cyber warfare command to protect its military computer systems, the plans are part of the ministry's strategy known as "Defense Reform 2020" [18]. The Korea Internet & Security Agency (KISA) was also formed.

On the North Korea side they have built capabilities under Unit: 121, which was stood up in 1998. The mission is to increase their military standing by advancing their asymmetric and cyber warfare capabilities through both offensive and espionage methods. This unit is trained by the Mirim Academy in Pyongyang. Their annual budget is estimated to be ~$56M [19]. With the struggle on the Korean peninsula still going on, it is easy to see why they would carry the battle to cyberspace. This could give North Korea an advantage as they are not as dependent on IT infrastructure as most countries, but at the same time they will have to come a long way to overcome the lack of a computer workforce to draw from.

Terrorists have no formal published doctrine but they are very interested in understanding the doctrine of the countries that they want to attack. It would be important to know what a countries response to specific attacks would be so they can plan which attacks will accomplish their objectives. They also have many locally developed doctrinal practices for reconnaissance, communication, and recruiting on the internet so they are leveraging the capabilities it offers. Finally, it should be assumed that they understand how many of the countries in the west depend on cyber so have actively sought out capabilities to exploit this vulnerability but to date no plans have been seen on how they would accomplish it.

European Countries

The Cooperative Cyber Defense Center of Excellence (CCD COE) located in Tallinn, Estonia, was formally established on the 14th of May, 2008, in order to enhance North Atlantic Treaty Organization's (NATO) cyber defense capabilities. The Center received full accreditation by NATO and attained the status of International Military Organization on the 28th of October, 2008. Its mission is to enhance the capability, cooperation, and information sharing among NATO, NATO nations and Partners in cyber defense by virtue of education, research and development, lessons learned, and consultation [20]. This center is designed to allow NATO to integrate cyber doctrine. There are political, legal, doctrinal, and technical issues that must be worked out when operating in a multi-national task force. It has taken years to develop the processes to do this in the real world and NATO is moving to establish the same functionality in the virtual world.

The United Kingdom is developing strategies and doctrine for cyber as well. The "Cybersecurity Strategy of the United Kingdom safety—security and resilience in cyber space" published in June 2009 by UK Office of Cybersecurity and UK Cybersecurity Operations Center. This document states there is an ongoing and broad debate regarding what "cyber warfare" might entail, but it is a point of consensus that with a growing dependence upon cyberspace, the defense and exploitation of information systems are increasingly important issues for national security. We recognize the need to develop military and civil capabilities, both nationally and with allies, to ensure we can defend against attack, and take steps against adversaries where necessary. Furthermore, these include criminals, terrorists, and states, whether for reasons of espionage, influence or even warfare [21]. This acknowledgement that cyber war is a distinct possibility and they are preparing for it is a clear statement that the UK is treating this as a matter of national security. They expanded the scope of cyber battle space to include criminals and espionage but treat them as separate from warfare, this inclusion in the statement shows the overlap that is one of the challenges in cyber doctrine.

France's government published a white paper on defense and national security which says Cyber war is a major concern for which the White Paper develops a two-pronged strategy: on the one hand, a new concept of cyber defense, organized in depth and coordinated by a new Security of Information Systems Agency under the purview of the General Secretariat for Defense and National Security; on the other hand, the establishment of an offensive cyber war capability, part of which will come under the Joint Staff and the other part will be developed within specialized services [22]. Though not a national strategy, this white paper does call out their belief that this is a military problem with the need for offensive capabilities under their special services units. They have followed the model that most countries are going to—stand up a new and separate organization to handle cyber war; very few are trying to integrate this capability into their traditional forces. This is the same pattern Space support went through before it was integrated into tactical operations on the battlefield.

The Czech Republic has published their cybersecurity strategy for 2011–2015. This states, "Essential objectives of the cybersecurity policy include protection against threats which information and communication systems and technologies (hereinafter "ICTs") are exposed to, and mitigation of potential consequences in the event of an attack against ICTs. The implementation, operation, and security of credible information and communication systems is a duty of the Czech Republic and a responsibility of all levels of government and administration, the private sector and the general public, the objective being to maintain a safe, secure, resistant, and credible environment that makes use of available opportunities offered by the digital age. The strategy focuses mainly on unimpeded access to services, data integrity, and confidentiality of the Czech Republic's cyberspace and is coordinated with other related strategies and concepts." It is worth noting they call on their general public as part of the solution [23].

Private or Mercenary Armies

In an age where cyber warfare is more common than the physical battlefield, it may be necessary for the private sector to stop playing defense and go on offense, Gen. Michael Hayden said on August 1, 2011. Hayden, who led the National Security Administration and Central Intelligence Agency under president George W. Bush, said during a panel discussion at the Aspen Security Forum in Aspen, Colo. that the federal government may not be the sole defender of private sector companies—and that there is precedent for such action. "We may come to a point where defense is more actively and aggressively defined even for the private sector and what is permitted there is something that we would never let the private sector do in physical space," he said. "Let me really throw out a bumper sticker for you: how about a digital Blackwater?" he asked. "I mean, we have privatized certain defense activities, even in physical space, and now you have got a new domain in which we donot have any paths trampled down in the forest in terms of what it is we expect the government—or will allow the government—to do" [24]. Blackwater is a private military contractor that has changed its name to Academi after incidents in Iraq gave them a negative image. If companies decide to hire forces (hackers) to strike back or conduct recovery operations it could change the cyberspace battlefield dramatically.

SOME KEY MILITARY PRINCIPLES THAT MUST BE ADAPTED TO CYBER WARFARE

There are a number of Tactics Techniques and Procedures (TTPs) that are used to implement doctrine. Some of the fundamental TTPs are Intelligence Preparation of the Operational Environment (IPOE), Force Analysis using Joint Munitions Effectiveness Manual (JMEM) factors, Measures of Effectiveness (MOEs), Battle Damage Assessment (BDA) to determine if MOEs were achieved, Close Air Support (CAS) to integrate air and land forces, and Counterinsurgency (COIN) to adapt classic force on force doctrine to asymmetric battlefield.

Intelligence Preparation of the Operational Environment (IPOE)

Intelligence Preparation of the Battlefield (IPB) has evolved to become Intelligence Preparation of the Operational Environment (IPOE) in today's complex wars. It is "the analytical process used by joint intelligence organizations to produce intelligence estimates and other intelligence products in support of the joint force commander's decision-making process. It is a continuous process that includes defining the operational environment; describing the impact of the operational environment; evaluating the adversary; and determining adversary courses of action" [1]. This requires evaluating both traditional enemy capabilities and terrain but also now includes many new demographics (i.e. economic, race, religious, gender, ethnic, and cultural). When looking at lines of communication, influence operation and terrain it is now necessary to include cyberspace in that analysis. Cyber IPOE is vital to keeping inside the enemies OODA loop (Observe / Orient / Decide / Act). "IPB must be: timely, accurate, usable, complete, and relevant to be useful. In most cases, the basic groundwork needs to be 80% complete before operations and logistics can start planning" [25]. So with terrain that can change by the minute, forces that can be spread across the world and motives as diverse as the groups involved IPOE must relook at how it produces products like "enemies most likely course of action" but these products are still vital to the commander and must not be ignored in cyberspace.

Joint Munitions Effectiveness Manual (JMEM)

Joint Munitions Effectiveness Manual (JMEM) is formal capabilities analysis that determines effectiveness of different weapon systems (i.e. can a AT4 bazooka destroy a T64 Tank). These estimates may be generated using probabilistic mathematical models that take into account the target's critical vulnerabilities, performance data on the assets contemplated for application against the target, and means of delivery or they can be done via field testing. These predictions are based on historical data using strike performance and analyses of likely success given the specific planned weapon / target pairings (i.e. Air-to-Surface, Special Operations Target Vulnerability, or Surface-to-Surface) [1]. This is fairly straightforward when measuring kinetic effects but there are a multitude of factors that can impact the effeteness of a cyber weapon. We need to establish a standard to measure effectives that is used for a baseline so a commander can understand which cyber munitions is best for their needs. The standard will be based on some type of effect like "time not available" or "ability to influence decision."

There has been some work on this under the title—JOINT NON-KINETIC EFFECTS INTEGRATION (JNKEI) which was completed on September 2010. The purpose was to develop joint TTPs to assist joint planners in integrating the non-kinetic effects of electronic attack, computer network attack, and offensive space control capabilities into operational planning. The following was accomplished:

- Improved integration of non-kinetic capabilities during operational planning that expand the range of possible courses of action for joint force commanders.
- Information exchange requirements based on the JNKEI TTPs and incorporated into the Integrated Strategic Planning and Analysis Network (ISPAN) and Virtual Integrated Support for the Information Operations Environment (VisIOn) collaborative tools.
- Input provided to Joint Publication (JP) 5-0, Joint Operational Planning; Joint Test Publication 3-12, Cyberspace Operations; JP 3-13, Information Operations; and JP 3-60, Joint Targeting.
- JNKEI TTPs provided to Joint Information Operations Planning Course (Joint Forces Staff College), Joint Targeting School (USJFCOM), and Advanced Integrated Warfighter Weapons Instructor Course (US Air Force Weapon School).
- JNKEI TTPs provided to USEUCOM; USPACOM; US Force, Korea; and USSTRATCOM to enhance existing standard operating procedures.

Measures of Effectiveness (MOE)

Measures of Effectiveness (MOEs) assess changes in system behavior, capability, or operational environment that is tied to measuring the attainment of an end state, achievement of an objective, or creation of an effect; they do not measure task performance. When evaluating a course of action or combat assessments we need to evaluate it based on the impact or MOE it will have. These MOEs should use assessment metrics that are relevant, measurable, responsive, and resourced so there is no false impression of task or objective accomplishment [1]. This can be very complex if we are talking about influence operations or information operations. We need to establish a standard by which every branch of the military and federal agencies measure both impact and effectives. It will need to be a matrix that can deal with compromise to confidentiality, denial of access, and loss of integrity that reflects the consequences to the aspect of national power that was effected (military, economic, information, or diplomatic). It should be done in an unclassified format so that everyone trains and uses it to the point it is universally understood.

Battle Damage Assessment (BDA)

Battle Damage Assessment (BDA) is another key TTP. It is the estimate of damage resulting from the application of lethal or non-lethal military force. Battle damage assessment is composed of physical damage assessment, functional damage assessment, and target system assessment. The purpose of BDA is to compare post-execution results with the projected/expected results generated during target development. Comprehensive BDA requires a coordinated and integrated effort between joint force intelligence and operations functions. Traditionally, BDA is composed of physical damage assessment, functional damage assessment, and functional assessment of the next higher target system [1]. BDA is vital to determining if the attack method has a successful MOE. The Air Force would not launch aircraft until they were sure the enemy's anti-aircraft batteries were destroyed. Cyber forces would not launch their exploit until they knew they could bypass the defensive firewalls. Generally, it is best to integrate all the different collection capabilities into "all source" information (allowing correlation acrossall the Intel Functions) to providing accurate analysis.

Close Air Support (CAS)

Close Air Support (CAS) is Air action by fixed- and rotary-wing aircraft against hostile targets that are in close proximity to friendly forces and that require detailed integration of each air mission with the fire and movement of those forces [1]. This TTP reminds us that combined forces are more powerful when they are integrated. The US does not fight wars alone—they fight as part of multinational coalitions, the Army rarely fights alone—they fight as part of a Joint Task Force and a cyber war will most likely be part of the integrated effort using multiple aspects of national power.

Counterinsurgency (COIN)

Counterinsurgency (COIN) is comprehensive civilian and military efforts taken to simultaneously defeat and contain insurgency, and address its core grievances. COIN is primarily political, and incorporates a wide range of activities, of which security is only one. Unified action is required to successfully conduct COIN operations and should include all Host Nation (HN), US, and multinational agencies or actors [1]. Combating insurgency is the most prevalent type of conflict the United States has been engaged in recent history. In this kind of environment Information Operations and Influence Operations are key force multipliers. Cyber is a critical weapon for both sides in this kind of fight. As commanders analyze how to fight and win on today's battlefield they must understand how to dominate cyberspace. The same tools they use to fight on the local terrain can be modified to be used in cyberspace if we force the staff functions to focus on the right requirements.

SUMMARY

This chapter has explored the state of current cyber warfare doctrine on both the nation state and military. Every country with a dependence on IT infrastructure is developing strategies and capabilities to protect and exercise national power. We then examined some of the traditional tactics and products that the military needs to adapt to the cyberspace environment. We covered some of the directives used by federal agencies and governments to guide behavior in this virtual environment. Finally we took a look at how organizations are training to both develop new doctrine and execute their current plans.

Today we are at the beginning of a new era of culture, individual and nation state influence, and possibly warfare (both economic and force on force conflicts). Governments and militaries all over the world are aggressively working on developing doctrine to defend, fight, and win in this new domain.

REFERENCES

[1] DoD. Joint Electronic Library. [online, cited: 09.07.2010]. <http://www.dtic.mil/doctrine/>.

[2] President Obama. The Comprehensive National Cybersecurity Initiative. [online] May 2011. <http://www.whitehouse.gov/cybersecurity/comprehensive-national-cybersecurity-initiative>.

[3] Gates, Secretary of Defense Robert. Wall Street Journal. Resource Documents. [online] DoD, June 23, 2009. <http://online.wsj.com/public/resources/documents/OSD05914.pdf>.

[4] Alexander General Keith B. Statement of commander United States cyber command before the house committee on armed services. September 23, 2010.

[5] Congressman W. Mac. Thornberry (R) Definitions, Focal Point, and Methodology Needed for DOD to Develop Full-Spectrum Cyberspace Budget Estimates. [online] July 2011. <http://www.gao.gov/products/GAO-11-695R>.

[6] Major General Richard E. Webber, USAF. US House of Representatives House Armed Services Committee. Presentation to the subcommittee on terrorism and unconventional threats. [online] US NAVY, September 23, 2010. <http://democrats.armedservices.house.gov/index.cfm/files/serve?File_id=8b28f10f-e164-481f-93cc-0c0734195fb1>.

[7] Dominance, VADM Jack Dorsett DCNO for Information. Information Dominance and the US Navy's Cyber Warfare Vision. The Defense Technical Information Center. [online] US Navy, April 14, 2010. <http://www.dtic.mil/ndia/2010SET/Dorsett.pdf>.

[8] Army, US. TRADOC pam 525-7-8. Cyberspace Operations Concept Capability Plan 2016–2028. February 22, 2010.

[9] Stew Magnuson Army Wants Ability to Fight in Cyberspace by 2020 [online] November 2011. <http://www.nationaldefensemagazine.org/blog/Lists/Posts/Post.aspx?ID=582>.

[10] Headlines Army's First Dedicated Cyber Brigade Now Operational [online] March 2012. <http://www.infosecisland.com/blogview/20751-Armys-First-Dedicated-Cyber-Brigade-Now-Operational.html>.

[11] TRICARE, DoD. TRICARE. Military Health System Information Assurance Guidance. [online] 10.10.2008. <http://www.health.mil/Libraries/ia-files/14-INFOCON-10102008.pdf>.

[12] Wiangsui, Qiao Liang and Wang. Unrestricted Warfare. Beijing: PLA Literature and Arts Publishing House, February 1999.

[13] Thomas, Timothy. Air Force Space Command High Frontier. Taiwan Examines Chinese Information Warfare. [online] Air Force, May 2009. <http://www.afspc.af.mil/shared/media/document/AFD-090519-102.pdf>.

[14] Krekel, Bryan. Capability of the People's Republic of China to Conduct Cyber Warfare and Computer Network Exploitation. The US-China Economic and Security Review Commission. [online] October 9, 2009. <http://www.uscc.gov/researchpapers/2009/NorthropGrumman_PRC_Cyber_Paper_FINAL_Approved%20Report_16Oct2009.pdf>.

[15] Associated Press 12 Chinese Hacker Teams Responsible for Most US Cybertheft. [online] December 2011. <http://www.foxnews.com/scitech/2011/12/12/12-chinese-hacker-teams-responsible-for-most-us-cybertheft/>.

[16] Strategy Page The Mighty 1st Technical Reconnaissance Bureau. [online] April 2011. <http://www.strategypage.com/htmw/htiw/articles/20110417.aspx>.

[17] Yasuhide Yamada, Atsuhiro Yamagish, Ben T. Katsumi. Comparative study of the information security policies of Japan and the United States. J Natl Security Law [online, cited: 17.09.2010]. <http://infosecmgmt.pro/sites/default/files/us-japan_information_security_comparison_4_yamada.pdf>.

[18] Yong-sup, Han. Analyzing South Korea's Defense Reform 2020. The Korean Journal of Defense Analysis, Vol. XVIII, No. 1, [online] Spring 2006. <http://kida.re.kr/data/kjda/06_1_5.pdf>.

[19] Jr., Joseph S. Bermudez. SIGINT, EW, and EIW in the Korean People's Army. Asia-Pacific Center for Security Studies. [online] 2005. <http://www.apcss.org/Publications/Edited%20Volumes/BytesAndBullets/CH13.pdf>.

[20] Cooperative Cyber Defence Centre of Excellence. NATO and attained the status of International Military Organisation. [online, cited: 10.17.2010]. <http://www.ccdcoe.org/12.html>.

[21] Centre, Office of Cyber Security and Cyber Security Operations. Cyber Security Strategy of the United Kingdom. Cabinet Office. [online] June 2009. <http://www.cabinetoffice.gov.uk/media/216620/css0906.pdf>.

[22] République, Présidence De La. The French White Paper on defence and national security. Le Livre blanc sur la défense et la sécurité nationale. [online] June 2007. <http://www.livreblancdefenseetsecurite.gouv.fr/IMG/pdf/white_paper_press_kit.pdf>.

[23] Czech Republic Czech Cyber Security Strategy for 2011–2015 published [online] August 2011. <http://www.enisa.europa.eu/media/news-items/czech-cyber-security-strategy-published>.

[24] Andrew Nusca Hayden Digital Blackwater may be necessary for private sector to fight cyber threats. [online] August 2011. <http://www.zdnet.com/blog/btl/hayden-digital-blackwater-may-be-necessary-for-private-sector-to-fight-cyber-threats/53639>.

[25] Winterfeld, Steve. GSEC Gold Credentials. Cyber IPB. [online] December 2001. <http://www.giac.org/paper/gsec/1752/cyber-ipb/103147>.

[9] Headlines Army's End, Designated Cyber Brigade Now Operational [online] March 2012, <http://www.afcea.org/blog/?p=9232> Army's First Dedicated Cyber Brigade Now Operational. http://

[10] TRICARE Data, TRICARE Military Health System Information Assurance Guidance [online] 10.10.2008, <http://www.health.mil/Reference/Policies+DoD/OCIO/p8580 pdf>.

[11] Wenyuan Qiao Liang and Wang, Unrestricted Warfare, Beijing: PLA Literature and Arts Publishing House, February 1999.

[12] Thomas, Timothy Air Force Space Command Flight Focused Threat Weather Center, Information Warfare Journal, Air Force, May 2009. <http://www.afspc.af.mil/library/>, monitor concept AFD-090519-102 pdf>.

[13] Krekel, Bryan, Capability of the People's Republic of China to Conduct Cyber Warfare and Computer Network Exploitation, The US-China Economic and Security Review Commission, [online] October 9, 2009, <http://www.uscc.gov/researchpapers/2009/NorthropGrumman_PRC_Cyber_Paper_FINAL_Approved%20Report_16Oct2009. pdf>.

[14] Associated Press, 12 Chinese Hacker Teams Responsible for Most US Cybertheft [online] December 2011, <http://www.foxnews.com/scitech/2011/12/12/12-chinese-hacker-teams-responsible-for-most-us-cybertheft>.

[15] Secure, Page the Mighty U-1 Technical Reconnaissance Bureau, [online] April 2011, <http://www.secureye.com/blog/whworldpl/w/2011/04/1-pj/jps>.

[16] Yasuhide Yamada, Atsuhiro Yamagishi, Ben T. Katsumi, Comparative study of the information security policies of Japan and the United States, Japan Security Law [online] e5xxx-17.00.2010], <http://pjlistcscms/int prochure/default/data/web/japan_information security comparison_4_e.pdf/>.

[17] Young-sup, Han, Analyzing South Korea's Defense Reform 2020, The Korean Journal of Defense Analysis, Vol. XVIII, No. 1, [online] Spring 2006, <http://www.idec.gov.tw/ida/xxxx>.

[19] L. Joseph S. Bermudez, SIGINT, EW, and IW in the Korean People's Army Aug., Facing Center for Security Studies, [online] 2005, <http://www.apcss.org/Publications/Edited%20volumes/SciencMdbfieldsCH13.pdf>.

[20] Cooperative Cyber Defense Center of Excellence, NATO and outlined the status of International Military Organisation, [online] cited 30.11.2010], <http://www.cdoe.org/223/html>.

[21] Centre, Office Of Cyber Security and other Security Coordinators, Cyber Security Strategy of the United Kingdom Cabinet Office [online] June 2009, <http://www.cabinetoffice.gov.uk/media/216620/css0906.pdf>.

[22] Republique, Presidential De La The French White Paper Defense and National Security, La Libre blanc sur la défense et la sécurité nationale, [online] June 2008 <http://www.livreblancdefensecourier.gouv fr/IMG/pdf/Shi Shaw_paper_press_kit.pdf>.

[23] Cen, in National Cyber Security Strategy SLO.K.v.TO2011. 2014 published [online] August 2011, <http://www.enisa.europa.eu/media/news-items/slovenian-defence-cyber-security-strategy-published>.

[24] Andrew, virus Hayden Hotel that would not be necessary for private sector to fight cyber threats, [online] August 2011 <http://www.secretxldsx.com/slovpublloov/en-digital-blackmail-camp-hack-camp-cassay-hue-private-sector-to-fight-cyberthreats-93-96>.

[25] Witte Heln Steve GSEC Gina Certification Cyber IWn, [online] December 2011, <http://www.iwsgivupbpl/sec41-79x1x1x/xxxxx10121425>.

Tools and Techniques

INFORMATION IN THIS CHAPTER:

- Logical Weapons
- Physical Weapons

LOGICAL WEAPONS

Logical weapons are the tools or software programs that we likely envision when discussing cyber warfare. These are the set of tools that is used to conduct reconnaissance, scout out the networks and systems of our opponents, and attack or exploit (which means to spy on in terms of CNE, as we will discuss further in Chapter 5) the various targets we might find. When we look at the use of such tools in a cyber warfare context, we might ask how they are different than the tools used in every day penetration testing of applications, systems, and networks. The answer to this is that, in many cases, they not conceptually different to any great degree, but the intent and impact of their use is often greatly increased in a cyber warfare scenario.

Where penetration testers may be bound, contractually in some cases, to shy away from the tools or settings in tools that are labeled "dangerous" due to their possible deleterious effects on the target at the other end, such effects may be acceptable, or even desirable in a cyber conflict. This may not always be the case, and we certainly may still want to be stealthy and cautious in some scenarios, but this opens up the use of the common tools in such a way that we do not normally see in penetration testing outside of a lab environment.

We may very well find commercial tools in the hands of cyber warfare forces that are backed by, or in the employ of, nation states, but we are less likely to find them in the hands of individuals or small groups. Nonetheless, in skilled hands, the free tools can be highly effective, if less automated than some of the commercial tools, and are used regularly by a variety of attackers.

> **NOTE**
>
> The selection of tools available for use in cyber warfare, penetration testing, and security in general is truly staggering. While a complete discussion of the various popular security tools would have been great to be able to include, we would have to devote an entire book to it to have been able to do so. It is also worth noting that while hackers may spend thousands some countries are spending billions (i.e. USA with National Security Agency and Comprehensive National Cybersecurity Initiative). In this chapter, we discuss a few of the highlights, but for those still wanting more, Insecure.org is a great place to look. They maintain lists of password crackers, sniffers, vulnerability scanners, web scanners, wireless tools, and numerous other tools of the trade.

Reconnaissance Tools

Reconnaissance tools, as should be clear from the name, are those that we use to gather information, usually in a passive state, about the networks and systems that we might plan to take action against in a logical sense. Such efforts may include gathering information from public websites, looking up Domain Name System (DNS) server records, collecting metadata from accessible documents, retrieving very specific information through the use of search engine, or any of a number of other similar activities. For reconnaissance, we may use information gathered from sources such as:

- Websites.
- Search engines.
- Google hacking.
- WHOIS searches/DNS queries.
- Metadata.
- Specialized search tools such as Maltego.

Scanning Tools

Scanning tools are the category of tools that we use to find more information about our target environment, the systems within it, and the details of those systems. With such tools, we can be very general, in the case of running ping sweeps, somewhat more specific, in the case of running port scans, or very specific, in the case of grabbing banners or enumerating users on particular systems. Some common tools used for scanning include:

- Nmap.
- Nessus.
- OpenVAS.

Access and Escalation Tools

A great number of the hacking and penetration testing tools available, both open source and commercial, are focused on gaining access to systems and escalating the level of privilege once we are able to access the system. We will cover some of the more common and more popular tools in this section. Common access and escalation tools might include:

- Password cracking/guessing tools.
- Metasploit.
- CANVAS.

Exfiltration Tools

Exfiltrating data from an environment can be an interesting and challenging problem, particularly if the environment in question is secured against exactly the activities that we are attempting to carry out. In broad strokes, some of the main methods that we can use to exfiltrate data are to physically carry the data out, to use steganography or encryption to disguise the data, to make use of common protocols that are normally allowed to leave the environment, or to use out-of-band methods. Some common methods of exfiltration include:

- Physical exfiltration.
- Encryption and/or steganography.
- Tunneling over common protocols.
- Out-of-band (OOB) methods.

Sustainment Tools

Once we have gained access to a system and reached the desired level of access, we will likely want to ensure that we can continue to access the system in the future. Although we may have been able to successfully use a particular vulnerability or similar means to access the system in the first place, we cannot necessarily depend on the same weakness to still exist in the future. Some common methods of sustaining access may include:

- Adding "authorized" accounts to systems.
- Backdoors.
- Adding listening services.

Assault Tools

The tools that can be used to assault a compromised machine are many and varied. They can take the form of simple changes to configurations or environment variables on a system, to purpose-built botnets that can conduct a concentrated Denial of Service (DoS) attack on a given system or environment. Such tools of destruction can generally be categorized into those related to software or oriented on hardware. Some common assault methods might include:

- Tampering with software or operating system settings.
- Attacking hardware.
- Changing configurations.

Obfuscation Tools

To obfuscate means to "confuse, bewilder, or stupefy," "to make obscure or unclear," or "to darken" [1]. This definition perfectly suits the set of tools that we might use to cover our tracks when operating on a system or in an environment. In general, there are three main types of tasks that we are concerned with in such cases: obscuring our location, manipulating logs, and manipulating files. Some methods of obfuscation might include:

- Obscuring physical location.
- Log manipulation.
- File manipulation.

PHYSICAL WEAPONS

When we think of cyber warfare, we most likely envision legions of über-nerds, staring intently at banks of monitors while madly typing away at their keyboards. While there may be some measure of truth to this particular mental picture, we also need to consider the place of conventional warfare in such conflicts.

When we look at how the physical and logical realms intersect, we find that they are very closely linked indeed. Logical systems, such as software and applications, are entirely dependent on the physical systems and infrastructure on which they run. Changes made to either the physical or logical components can have profound effects on each other, with one sometimes rendering the other completely useless.

Just as in any large conflict of a physical nature, we are also concerned with the infrastructure and the supply chain or logistics that make our operations possible. If either of these components is removed or subverted by opposing forces, conducting warfare becomes considerably more difficult, at best. At worst, we may find ourselves unable to act entirely, nullified by supply chain issues such as food poisoning from a batch of contaminated egg salad in a mess hall or cafeteria, or subverting the components used in assembling electronic or computing devices.

When looking at the tools we can use for physical attack and defense, we have a wide variety of options available to us. We can use conventional explosives, cut cables, jam transmissions, pick locks, and nearly anything else that springs to our imaginations. For defense, we can harden our facilities and equipment against the attacks that we consider to be the most likely, and we can take steps to ensure that those attackers that do make it through our perimeter are frustrated in their attempts and quickly detected.

How the Logical and Physical Realms are Connected

The concept that the logical realm depends on physical hardware and network infrastructure is an generally understood by those with a basic degree of technical knowledge. Though the idea of the virtual world riding on the physical world is indeed a simple one, some of the second order effects of intersections between these two worlds may not be as clear or immediately obvious.

When looking at the physical network infrastructure on which such systems are maintained, we have two primary issues to consider in cyber operations; keeping our own systems and infrastructure intact and able to function as designed, and rendering the opposing systems and infrastructure unable to do so. This means that a physical attack on the data center is an option for military denial of service attacks.

Logical systems can also be used to make changes in the physical world. In complex items of physical hardware, software often regulates the way that the hardware functions. Changes made to the software can affect whatever the hardware interfaces with, including networks, other systems, or even people. This means a cyber attack against the energy grid can be used as a denial of service against the data center as well.

Logical Systems Run on Physical Hardware

The logical world runs on a variety of network infrastructure, computer systems, home automation devices, refrigerators, cars, and so on (generally called embedded devices). When such a complex device loses connection to the various utilities that are critical to its functionality, mainly power and communications media, it becomes considerably less useful, often times to the point of being rendered a very expensive paperweight.

When conducting operations in a cyber conflict, whether offensive or defensive, keeping the physical hardware running that enables such activity can be challenging. Even in conventional warfare, an element of advanced technology has begun to enter the fray, and the intelligence provided by such technology can provide critical information on which to base cyber, as well as conventional, operations.

Many recent actions in which the United States has participated, such as those in Iraq and Afghanistan, have taken place in desert locations that tend to be very hot and sandy, with little existing infrastructure to speak of. Operating in such environments tends to be less than optimal for the continued functionality of computing equipment. In addition, such equipment may pose a tempting target for opposing forces to attack, both on a physical and a logical level as they are the key to US command and control. In such cases, ruggedized equipment and portable cooling systems are often required in order to have any expectation for the devices to function over a period of time.

Additionally, at a higher level, we need to keep the infrastructure working for such systems to utilize. Such technology is commonly found in data centers and other areas that house critical computing equipment, although it is not commonly hardened to withstand the levels of attack that we might find in a cyber conflict. By using redundant systems, infrastructure, utilities, and other such necessities, we can make it very difficult to take systems down. On the other hand, since such technologies are generally available, we will likely find them implemented by our opponents as well.

On the reverse side of this issue is the problem of attempting to render the equipment and infrastructure of the opposing forces inoperable from a physical perspective. Particularly when physical operations are being conducted on foreign soil, those under attack may have a distinct "home court" advantage. In some situations, such as the conflict in Afghanistan, we may be dealing with an opponent that does not rely on a sophisticated technological infrastructure at all. In other cases, we may be facing well-constructed data centers that are hardened and have sufficient backup resources to provide power and communications in emergencies. These can prove to be very difficult to take offline. Each enemy theater of operation will have a blend of dependency and ability to support net-centric operations and must be evaluated separately.

During Operation Iraqi Freedom in 2003, several rounds of cruise missiles were required to disrupt the Internet access in Baghdad. Although the civilian Internet Service Providers (ISPs) were taken down with relative ease, with much of the traffic originating from behind a single Cisco switch, the traffic coming from the Iraqi government was not so easily silenced. After direct hits on two telecommunications switching centers, several satellite dishes, and a server housed in the Iraqi Ministry of Information building, the official Iraqi government website and the associated email server were taken offline. It later appeared that communications were being carried through a satellite gateway that had been shipped to Dubai by the manufacturer, and later brought into Iraq [2]. This shows the difficultly in mapping threats in the cyber environment and key infrastructure nodes.

Given the ease of constructing backup systems on a variety of infrastructures, it is entirely possible that multiple systems would need to be taken down to remove the cyber capability of an opponent. Internet access can be provided over microwave, cell, ham radio, phone lines, and a variety of other solutions, and can be shared through mesh networking to enable a great degree of redundancy. Given today's technologics a system could even be made to function at a minimal level from a laptop and a data connection from a cell phone. In such cases, a combination of physical and logical attacks may be required to completely take a system offline.

Logical Attacks Can Have Physical Effects

Just as physical attacks can affect logical systems, logical attacks can affect physical systems. To a great extent, physical computing systems are controlled by the operating systems and applications that are running on them. As a very simple example, for almost all systems that are physically connected to a network cable, changes to the network configuration can be made in such a way as to remove the device from the network.

> **TIP**
> Web administration interfaces are wonderful for knocking devices off of the network. They often have poor security, if the security features have been enabled on them at all. Although they have relatively limited functionality in most cases, many of them do have the capability to change basic network settings. Typically an attack as simple as setting the IP address on such a device to 0.0.0.0 will disable its network functionality handily.

In the case of such a device being removed from the network, a backup communications method could potentially be used to restore communications to the device, or a person will be required to physically travel to the device to reconfigure it. Such an attack may be very simple and ultimately very easy to fix, but using it to disrupt network infrastructure across an enterprise could bring an entire organization to a halt in very short order, and be very time consuming to fix. Additionally secondary communications systems are normally not as secure and could lead to opening the command up to espionage.

Attacks on physical systems can also have effects of a much more serious nature that can go far beyond merely annoying network and system administrators. In 2008, a team of security researchers, with the assistance of the University of Washington and the University of Massachusetts, were able to gain access to the unencrypted wireless signal used to control a combination defibrillator and pacemaker. Using this access they were able to alter the settings causing it to deliver potentially fatal shocks and to shut down entirely [3]. The attacks carried out in this line of research were decidedly non-trivial; requiring considerable amounts of research and specialized hardware, but the concept has now been proven. To make matters even worse for future attacks along these lines, in 2009 the first wireless and Internet connected pacemaker was installed in a patient [4]. To revisit our example above, remotely connecting to and disabling all such devices under the control of a particular doctor, a cardiologist at the White House, for instance, might have quite a profound effect in the political world.

In addition to such concerns around generic computing devices, these attacks can also be used to affect the critical systems that control the components running industrial processes around the world. Such systems control the distribution of power and water, communications systems, manufacturing, and any number of other important processes.

Infrastructure Concerns

When we mention the word infrastructure in the company of those that work in the computing and technology worlds, the common tendency is to assume that we are referring specifically to network infrastructure. While this infrastructure is indeed important and many processes would be completely non-functional without it, it is only a portion of the infrastructure on which the industrial world runs.

Of chief concern when we discuss infrastructure and the associated systems are the systems that actually control these items. These control systems regulate power, water, communications, manufacturing processes, and any number of other tasks. Properly referred to, such systems are Industrial Control Systems (ICS). ICS are made up of Supervisory Control and Data Acquisition (SCADA) systems, Distributed Control System (DCS), Human-Machine Interfaces (HMIs), Master Terminal Units (MTUs), Programmable Logic Controllers (PLCs), Remote Terminal Units (RTUs), Intelligent Electronic Devices (IEDs), and other such items [5].

These categories are often grouped together under the umbrella of SCADA, rather than calling them by the less familiar term ICS. In essence, the distinction between SCADA and ICS revolves around the specifics of where and what is actually being controlled or coordinated. In many cases, such distinctions are not standard between industries, and the term SCADA is often used where ICS may be more accurate in a technical sense.

What is SCADA?

Supervisory Control and Data Acquisition (SCADA) systems are used to control and monitor a variety of processes. Such processes can be industrial, infrastructure, or facility based [6]. Industrial processes can involve manufacturing facilities, generation of power, petroleum refineries, mining, or any number of similar activities that take place in factory-like environments. Infrastructure processes revolve around water and wastewater systems, pipelines used to distribute petroleum and natural gas, the transmission of electrical power, communications systems such as landline or cellular phone systems, and other systems that provide good and services that are commonly considered to be utilities. Facility processes are those that regulate processes in individual facilities such as heating and air conditioning, or energy usage. The military is starting to develop plans to deal with attacks against SCADA systems that key bases/forts depend on. One program is called Smart Power Infrastructure Demonstration for Energy Reliability and Security (SPIDERS).

SCADA systems are integrated into nearly everything that we come into contact with. While we are putting gas in our cars, surfing the web, cooking dinner, or flushing the toilet, we are only steps away from such systems, if not directly interacting with them. Remote sensors have become increasingly common in many residential areas, as it enables utility companies to gain greater accuracy in meter reading, and does not require a person to manually visit each reader in order to collect information from it. They are also being used in medical devices like pacemakers, hip replacements, and insulin pumps which wireless report back to medical staff. And finally there are CPUs in just about every weapon the US military uses today. All of these open up new threat vectors.

Without such systems to maintain and monitor the modern world, we would quickly be without heat, food, communications, and many other necessities. Needless to say, although such systems are designed for industrial usage and, in some critical systems, are multiply redundant, they are based on computer technology and therefore vulnerable.

What Security Issues are Present in the World of SCADA?

A large portion of the systems that fall under the category of SCADA depend on security through obscurity [7]. These systems use interfaces, software, operating systems, and protocols that are not generally well known outside of the industries in which they are implemented. In theory, in order for an attacker to penetrate a SCADA system, they would either need inside knowledge of the design for the particular, and potentially unique, system, or they would need to spend the time gaining access to and learning how things worked in order to carry out their attack.

Unfortunately, we are well into the information age, and a vast store of information awaits those willing to venture into the wasteland that we call the Internet. Manufacturers conveniently put manuals online for their customers to download, internal materials leak out to the public, and odd industrial systems can be bought for pennies on eBay. Although such systems do tend to be considerably more customized than the average server, we are well beyond the point of being able to depend on the obscure nature of a system conveying any large measure of protection against attackers. Indeed, systems and software that have not had the trial by fire of exposure to the Internet and outside attackers may very well be weaker for lack of having had their security flaws pointed out to the manufacturer.

As a case in point, in July of 2010 a multi-part malware named Stuxnet was discovered and its main target is SCADA systems. Stuxnet is composed of a worm which spreads over USB drives via a Windows exploit, and a Trojan which specifically looks for a particular model of Siemens SCADA systems. Also included is a rootkit to prevent its discovery. If Stuxnet finds that it is on the Siemens systems, it uses a hard-coded password to access the database that the SCADA system uses as a back end. It then looks for industrial automation layout files and control files and uploads them to a remote system, as well as attempting various acts of sabotage. Stuxnet then waits for additional commands from the remote system [8].

Stuxnet has been found in SCADA systems in a number of countries, including China, India, Iran, and Indonesia, with a possible point of origination in Israel. At first it appeared that the goal of the malware was industrial espionage. It was later discovered that Stuxnet attempted to actively sabotage such systems under certain circumstances, and may have been responsible for the loss of an Indian communications satellite [9]. In addition to such threats, as SCADA systems become more commonly connected to public and private networks, we are then exposed to the standard types of attacks with which many common systems are concerned. Distributed denial of service attacks (DDoS), side effects from malware attacks, patches that introduce security vulnerabilities, and a host of others now become issues for SCADA systems.

What are the Consequences of SCADA Failures?

In the case of serious SCADA failures, the potential consequences are quite far reaching. Considering that we are referring to the control systems for electrical power, communications, the flow of petroleum, and other such critical processes, a major disaster resulting from a SCADA failure seems likely indeed. We saw an example of the potential for such a failure during a large scale power blackout in 2003.

In parts of the US and Canada, in August of 2003, we saw the outcome from a SCADA failure that would, at first, seem to be relatively minor in nature, involving electrical distribution. Ultimately, a failure in a software monitoring system at a utility company in Ohio led to an outage at a local power plant. The failure of the power plant caused power to be drawn from other power plants in the area. Heavily loaded power lines, as seen in such outages, tend to physically sag, which several did. Sagging lines at multiple locations came into contact with improperly trimmed trees, causing these lines to also fail. While these failures were taking place, operators at the utility companies in Ohio neglected to inform controllers at utility systems in the surrounding states.

At that point, the utility systems in Ohio begin to draw power from the systems in Michigan, causing numerous issues as the system attempted to balance its load. Additional lines failed in Ohio and Michigan, causing power generating stations to go offline due to the absence of a load on them. Additional power was routed from plants on the east coast as the system continued to attempt to balance itself, causing plants on the east coast to overload, and shut down. Due to the massive power grid issues, grids in Michigan and Ohio began to disconnect from each other. Connections to Canada also began to fail, and instabilities in the grid caused grids in Canada to begin disconnecting as well. Ultimately, grids in Ontario, New York, New England, Windsor, New Jersey, and Philadelphia were affected [10].

At the end of the blackout 256 power plants were offline and 55 million customers were without power [11]. If we look all the way back at the beginning of the problem, the failure of a single monitoring system led to this enormous issue. Such situations have the potential for enormous loss of life and destruction, depending on the industry in which we see the failure. The blackout of 2003 was ultimately the result of a software bug, but was entirely accidental and those lessons have many militaries evaluating impacts. Given the attention of a determined opponent, such attacks have the potential for great disruption and destruction.

Supply Chain Concerns

In addition to the infrastructure concerns that we discussed above, awareness of our supply chain is also critical. We are now many years into a process of globalization that extends across nearly every large industry we might care to examine. Many countries import hardware and components to build infrastructure, a wide variety of foodstuffs, both processed and fresh, fuel, raw materials, clothing, and a number of other items, large and small, that are far too extensive to enumerate.

While this has a number of benefits, it also poses severe problems, particularly when we look at the possibilities of warfare in either the conventional or cyber sense. When we look at the infrastructure that we might rely on to conduct such attacks, or in the reverse situation, the infrastructure that might be under attack, the majority of the components, from individual items of equipment, all the way to the components from which they are constructed; almost all of these come from a few major manufacturing areas around the globe.

Compromised Hardware

Of major concern is the specter of hardware that has been compromised for strategic or intelligence purposes. Critical items, such as routers or switches, firewall appliances, industrial control units, or any of a number of other components may be deliberately engineered to clandestinely report information, fail given a particular signal or set of conditions, include a backdoor, or any number of other similar activities. This can place the party suffering such attacks at a distinct disadvantage, if not cripple their capacity to operate entirely.

In the late 1970s and early 1980s the US Central Intelligence Agency (CIA) learned of plans by the Russian Committee for State Security (KGB) to steal plans for a SCADA control system and its associated software from a Canadian company. Allegedly, the CIA was able to insert malware into the software for the system, which was later used in a trans-Siberian gas pipeline. In 1982 a massive explosion is reported to have taken place as a direct result of the flawed control system install [12]. There is some debate as to the validity of this report, but it does nicely illustrate the point.

To illustrate the ease of introducing such modified hardware into the market, we can look at the case of Operation Cisco Raider, a two-year investigation run by the US Federal Bureau of Investigation (FBI). In this operation, the FBI broke up a counterfeiting ring that had sold equipment to, among others, the US Navy, US Marine Corps, US Air Force, the US Federal Aviation Administration (FAA), and the FBI itself [13]. While this example was not based on military intent it shows another example of what could be done and is having some economic impact which erodes the US's overall powerbase.

In this particular case, the aim of the counterfeiting ring was profit rather than sabotage or espionage, and the amount of equipment concerned was very large. Under more stealth-focused circumstances, it is exceedingly unlikely that a few pieces of equipment that carried modified chips would be found, even given the government programs in place to do exactly this. We will discuss this issue in further depth, as well as some of the potential solutions, in Chapter 8.

Deliberately Corrupted Components

In addition to the specifically targeted and timed attacks that we discussed above, a much more simple supply chain issue can be brought about with the introduction of deliberately inferior or corrupted components. Particularly when looking at equipment with electronic components, this is a very easy type of attack to carry out. Considering the wide variety of components found in a typical item of electronic equipment and the large number of vendors that such components come from, such failures would be trivial to introduce and would be very wide reaching.

A specific case of an enormous number of issues related to a single bad component is that of the "capacitor plague" [14] that started in the late 1990s. A large portion of the issue relates to industrial espionage between capacitor manufacturers. Reportedly, the formula for the electrolyte used in capacitor manufacturing was stolen from a Japanese company and resold to several Taiwanese capacitor manufacturers. Unknown to any of the thieves, the formula was incomplete and lacked several key additives that would normally keep the capacitor from bursting. While this allowed the capacitors to function for a short period of time, it caused them to fail at generally less than half of their expected lifetime. According to some, this problem is still being seen in the market, with devices that have been produced nearly a decade after the original issue [15].

In this particular case, the issue was caused by an effort on the part of the legitimate manufacturer of the capacitors, as a defense mechanism against the theft of their intellectual property, and only got out of hand because the information was spread so widely. If this were a deliberate attempt at disrupting the supply chain of electronics components, it would be possible to produce components that were designed to fail in a very specific way, or at a particular time, as we covered in the previous section "Compromised Hardware." Such components could potentially find their way into missiles, tracking systems, aircraft avionics, or any number of other critical systems.

Non-Technical Issues

Of course when discussing supply chain issues, there are measures that could be used as attacks that do not directly relate to items of technology. Numerous issues relating to the supplies needed to conduct cyber warfare could present themselves to a sufficiently determined opponent and could prove profoundly effective at preventing such operations from being carried out. Additionally, given the potential for conducting such operations from centralized locations, such disruptions might be trivially easy to plan and implement.

In the words of Napoleon Bonaparte, "An army marches on its stomach" [16]. The consumable supplies that are necessary for our forces to conduct operations whether they are toothpaste, cold medicine, drinking water, food, or other such items, are all susceptible to contamination, whether deliberate or otherwise. We have seen many examples of the outcome of such events in countries around the globe.

In August of 2006, one particular brand of spinach was found to be contaminated with E. coli O157:H7. Throughout the end of August, the month of September, and the beginning of October, 199 people in 26 states became ill from eating the contaminated spinach, with 51% of the cases requiring hospitalization [17]. This particular case was accidental in nature, but still had very wide reaching consequences. If such contamination were to be deliberately carried out, particularly in a centralized location such as a cafeteria, an entire group of people could be incapacitated or worse.

Similar issues can appear with nearly any item that is required to support out forces, both conventional and cyber, particularly in locations that are not considered to be on the front lines of a particular engagement. Security in a protected remote location is likely to be much more lax than that found on any battlefield. Intentionally created supply issues are more likely, when carried out carefully and subtly, to be attributed to chance, rather than an outright attack.

Tools for Physical Attack and Defense

As we look at some of the conventional tools or weapon systems used for offense we turn to direct fire weapons like machineguns and tanks, and indirect weapons like artillery and jets. For defense we think of defensive mine fields and dug in troops. If we switch to reconnaissance we consider tools like satellite imaging, espionage or spies, and sending out scouts. The same concepts that apply to the physical aspects of the battlefield also apply to the cyber battlefield.

Electromagnetic Attacks

Electromagnetic attacks can be very useful in an environment where cyber conflicts are taking place and are part of integrated operations that include cyber. As such operations often depend on relatively delicate electronics, we can use this to our advantage. Such equipment can be affected by electromagnetic pulse (EMP) weapons, transmissions can be jammed, and emanations from such equipment can be eavesdropped upon.

Electromagnetic Pulse (EMP) Weapons

EMP weapons are a somewhat common player in movies, such as Oceans 11 and the Matrix, and books, but not quite as common in the real world. EMP weapons work by creating a very intense energy field which is very disruptive to non-hardened electronics. Such devices do exist in military arsenals, generally in the form of High Altitude Electromagnetic Pulse (HEMP) or High Power Microwave (HPM) weapons.

HEMP devices produce an EMP over a wide area, commonly produced by detonating a nuclear device high in the atmosphere. Obviously, if we are to the point of countries lobbing nuclear devices into the sky, things have gotten rather out of hand in the world of warfare, and we will likely have other concerns than cyber attacks in fairly short order. The more realistic scenario, at present, for such a device being used is as an act of terrorism. As shown in Figure 4.1, a HEMP device triggered at 300 miles altitude over central North America would affect an area covering most of the continent [18].

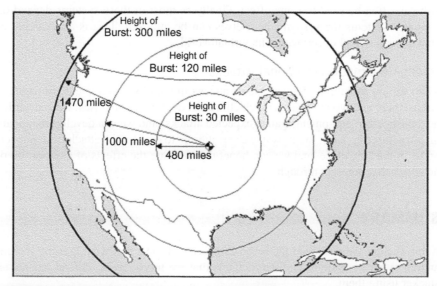

FIGURE 4.1 Estimated Area Affected by High Altitude EMP

WARNING

As civilians, intentional jamming of or interference with communications devices can often be found in the company of rather still penalties, depending on location. We should be careful to find out the legal particulars before engaging in such activities.

HPM devices can produce a similar effect, although on a smaller scale and with smaller equipment. Instead of needing a nuclear device, a HPM can use chemical explosives or very powerful batteries, in conjunction with a type of coil called a flux compression generator, to produce a powerful pulse. HPM devices can also limit the effect of the pulse produced to a smaller area over a shorter distance. Additionally, the pulse produced by the HPM is much more effective against electronics and is more difficult to harden devices against [18]. This is an example of physical denial of service.

Jamming

Particularly in many forces of a military nature, jamming technologies can be quite advanced. This set of technologies generally falls under the heading of Electronic Warfare (EW). EW systems can be used to jam nearly anything that utilizes the electromagnetic spectrum including radio, radar, sonar, infrared, laser, and a host of other technologies. Such technologies are very complex and expensive, but are common to many militaries.

On the other end of the spectrum, jamming can also be done very simply. Radio equipment can often be repurposed to interfere with transmission and receiving on other equipment, and plans for purpose-built home-brewed jamming equipment can be found on the Internet. Additionally, appliances such as portable phones, microwaves, and items that operate in the general area of the frequency to be interfered with can often be used to some effect. Finally as most of these systems depend on computer systems the systems themselves can be attacked. This is an example of what we call denial of service in the virtual world.

Defense Against Conventional Attacks

When we are looking to defend against attacks in the physical and electromagnetic realms, there are two main areas in which we can deploy our defenses; we can harden the facilities and equipment against expected attacks, and we can develop redundant infrastructures in place. In this way we can attempt to prevent the attack from impacting us in the first place, and we can hopefully mitigate the effects of any portion of the attack that does get through.

SUMMARY

In this chapter we discussed the broad categories of tools that we might use in conducting cyber operations, and the methods that we might use to defend against an attacker using them.

We also covered the use of physical weapons in cyber warfare. We talked about the intersection of the physical and logical realms and how making changes to either realm can affect the other, sometimes to a disastrous extent.

REFERENCES

[1] Dictionary.com. Obfuscate. *Dictionary.com*; 2010 [online, cited May 28, 2010, 2012]. <http://dictionary.reference.com/browse/obfuscate>.

[2] McWilliams Brian. Iraq goes offline. *Salon.com*; March 31, 2003 [online, cited May 28, 2010, 2012]. <http://dir.salon.com/story/tech/feature/2003/03/31/iraq_offline/index.html>.

[3] Pacemakers and implantable cardiac defibrillators: software radio attacks and zero-power defenses. In: Daniel Halperin et al., s.l., 2008 IEEE symposium on security and privacy; 2008.

[4] Reuters. New York woman receives wireless pacemaker. *PCMag.com*; August 10, 2009 [online, cited May 28, 2012]. <http://www.pcmag.com/article2/0,2817,2351371,00.asp>.

[5] Stouffer Keith, Falco Joe, Ken Karen. Guide to supervisory control and data acquisition (SCADA) and industrial control systems security; 2006.

[6] Juniper Networks, Inc. Architecture for secure SCADA and distributed control system networks; 2009. <http://www.juniper.net/us/en/local/pdf/whitepapers/2000276-en.pdf>.

[7] A plan for SCADA security to deter DoS attacks. In: Calvery Bowers, Timothy Buennemeyer, Ryan Thomas, s.l., Proceedings of the Department of Homeland Security: R&D partnering conference; 2005.

[8] Mills Elanor. Details of the first-ever control system malware. *Cnet New*; July 21, 2010 [online, cited May 28, 2012]. <http://news.cnet.com/8301-27080_3-20011159-245.html>.

[9] Woodward Paul. Israel: smart enough to create Stuxnet and stupid enough to use it. War in context; October 1, 2010 [online, cited May 28, 2012]. <http://warincontext.org/2010/10/01/israel-smart-enough-to-create-stuxnet-and-stupid-enough-to-use-it/>.

[10] US-Canada power system outage task force. Final report on the August 14, 2003 Blackout in the United States and Canada: causes and reccomendations; 2004. <https://reports.energy.gov/BlackoutFinal-Web.pdf>.

[11] Highleyman WH. The Great 2003 Northeast Blackout and the $6 billion software Bug. s.l., The availability digest; 2007. <http://www.availabilitydigest.com/private/0203/northeast_blackout.pdf>.

[12] Weiss Gus. The farewell Dossier. Central Intelligence Agency; June 27, 2008 [online, cited May 28, 2012]. <https://www.cia.gov/library/center-for-the-study-of-intelligence/csi-publications/csi-studies/studies/96unclass/farewell.htm>.

[13] Lawson Stephen, McMillian Robert. FBI worried as DoD sold counterfeit Cisco gear. InfoWorld Security Central; May 12, 2008 [online, cited May 28, 2012]. <http://www.infoworld.com/d/security-central/fbi-worried-dod-sold-counterfcit-cisco-gear-266>.

[14] Passalacqua Chris. How to identify. Badcaps.net; 2010 [online, cited May 28, 2012]. <http://www.badcaps.net/pages.php?vid=5>.

[15] Moore Samuel. Leaking capacitors muck up motherboards. IEEE Spectrum; February 2003 [online, cited May 28, 2012]. <http://spectrum.ieee.org/computing/hardware/leaking-capacitors-muck-up-motherboards/0>.

[16] Moore Richard. Maxims of Napoleon Bonaparte: on war. Napoleonic guide; 1999 [online, cited May 28, 2012]. <http://www.napoleonguide.com/maxim_war.htm>.

[17] National Center for Infectious Diseases. Update on multi-state outbreak of *E. coli* O157:H7 infections from fresh spinach; October 6, 2006. Centers for Disease Control and Prevention; October 6, 2006 [online, cited May 28, 2012]. <http://www.cdc.gov/ecoli/2006/september/updates/100606.htm>.

[18] Wilson Clay. High altitude electromagnetic pulse (HEMP) and high power microwave (HPM) devices: threat assessments. s.l., Congressional Research Service; 2008. <http://www.fas.org/sgp/crs/natsec/RL32544.pdf>. RL32544.

Offensive Tactics and Procedures

INFORMATION IN THIS CHAPTER:

- Computer Network Exploitation
- Computer Network Attack

COMPUTER NETWORK EXPLOITATION

The term Computer Network Exploitation (CNE) is a cyber warfare term of military origin, and one that may be slightly confusing to those that are not immediately familiar with the concept. While we might be tempted to think that the "exploit" in CNE refers to exploits used against systems in order to gain privileges or remote shells on them, this is not the case. In actuality, exploit in this case refers to the ability to exploit the data or information gathered on our target for our own purposes. Officially defined, CNE is "Enabling operations and intelligence collection capabilities conducted through the use of computer networks to gather data from target or adversary automated information systems or networks [1]." Such operations are the cyber equivalent of good old-fashioned spying. CNE is the phase of cyber warfare that we are experiencing globally at this point. We commonly see cyber reconnaissance and surveillance activities taking place, but we do not yet commonly see outright cyber attacks between nation-states.

Intelligence and Counter-Intelligence

Identifying who exactly the enemy is for purposes of CNE can be a bit of a tricky proposition. In the virtual world, when we refer to an enemy or opponent, we may actually be referring to what really are the second or third order effects of the actual activity of our opponent, or even beyond. In other words, when we see a Distributed Denial of Service (DDoS) attack coming from a group of machines in China, it is important to understand that the Chinese may not be related to the attack at all, other than in the sense of being an endpoint. To truly identify the enemy, we need to look at the targets, sources, attackers, and sponsors of the activity that we are monitoring.

Reconnaissance

Cyber reconnaissance can be divided into three major categories, Open Source Intelligence (OSINT), passive reconnaissance, and Advanced Persistent Threat (APT). While these three methods of reconnaissance are, for the most part, diametrically opposed, they all have their place in cyber warfare. We often will want to start with the use of OSINT to gather as much information as we can without directly indicating our interest, then proceed to passive reconnaissance when we need to gather more specific information that we have not been able to gain through the passive route.

Open Source Intelligence

OSINT involves the use of methods that are designed to not alert our target to the fact that they are under observation. Many of the tools that we discussed in the reconnaissance tools section of Chapter 4 fall squarely into this category. Investigating DNS information, Google hacking, information gathered from websites, investigation of document metadata, and other similar methods can all be excellent means of executing OSINT operations, as long as we are careful to not expose our interests in the process of conducting them. In OSINT we will likely start with public information, then job-related information, then Google hacking, then DNS information, then metadata gathering. When conducting reconnaissance against a target we will generally start with OSINT, and then move to passive.

Primarily, when taking an OSINT approach to reconnaissance, we will want to use information sources that do not leak information about our interests, or at least minimize such leakage. For instance, although we may use a public web-based whois query tool to conduct research against a target, the administrators of such an application may find it interesting that the IP address block of a known government contract organization had a suddenly high level of interest in the DNS information of systems related to the Chinese government. In such cases, it is often best to use a network masking technology such as The Onion Router (Tor), and to spread such queries out over many different sources.

To a certain extent, we can also use some network monitoring techniques for OSINT purposes. While we are very limited in what we can do for sniffing on a wireless network when bound by the requirement of stealth, there are packet sniffing

---

TIP

Tor, which can be found at www.torproject.org, is a tool that provides network anonymization by routing the traffic from a client through a variety of intermediate systems and out through one of many possible endpoints. Although Tor does indeed provide some measure of protection against a target or application being able to trace back the source of the network traffic in question, there are several attacks and configuration issues, including end points set up specifically to sniff traffic that may make it possible to do exactly this. This tool is downloadable from their site and can be added on most operating systems.

tools that are entirely passive in nature and are very difficult to detect without taking specific measures to do so.

There are also methods of network sniffing tools that work through induction rather than direct interface with the network that are, in theory, truly impossible to detect without physically finding the inductive tap itself [2]. Even fiber optic cables, often considered to not be passively tappable, in fact are exactly that. Low cost devices are available to read the light leakage through the jacket of a fiber cable without actually needing to cut it to insert a tap [3].

Additionally, we can eavesdrop on wireless network traffic in relative safety, as long as we are careful not to interact with the network itself. Even encrypted wireless traffic can reveal information about the devices that are connecting to it and, based off of names and Media Access Control (MAC) addresses of such devices, we can often infer quite a bit of information about the environment.

Passive Reconnaissance

Passive reconnaissance takes more direct steps to extract information on our target environment that OSINT does, but is passive in relation to the actual target. A good example of an attack being passive relative to the specific target might be compromising a router used by the target, then disrupting or degrading other paths in order to channel packets to the compromised router where we might more easily eavesdrop on the traffic. In such a case, we have altered the environment to aid in our reconnaissance, but have not touched the target itself.

Passive reconnaissance will often involve many of the tools that we discussed in Chapter 4 that involve directly interrogating a network or system, in order to discover its particulars or can be custom built by the attacker. Passive reconnaissance will often be, as we discussed, the next step OSINT and may be partially based on the information gathered during that activity. During passive reconnaissance, the defender may unintentionally expose information to our target from the nodes that are active in these tasks. In this way passive reconnaissance may differ greatly in cyber warfare activity than in penetration testing.

As for the tool likely to be used in passive reconnaissance, there are various scanning tools, such as network sniffers for both wired and wireless networks, port scanners, vulnerability analysis tools, operating system fingerprinting tools, banner grabbing tools, and other similar utilities. We will be looking to enumerate the infrastructure devices, networks, and systems in place in the environment, assess the ports open and services operating on those ports, fingerprint operating systems, and assess vulnerabilities. This process is certainly not set in stone and is intended as a general guideline. There will be times when a chain of interesting information will lead us to one step sooner than another and there is absolutely nothing wrong with varying the approach.

We will often find our future actions or attacks will enjoy a much greater degree of success if we take the time to carefully document the information discovered regarding the specifics of our target environment. This documentation will not only ease the planning of future attacks or more detailed reconnaissance, but will also ensure that all of those involved in the operation are working from the same set of information. It is also important to keep this documentation up to date as new information is gained, or as changes in the environment are noted.

Surveillance

The major difference between reconnaissance and surveillance is that reconnaissance tends to imply a single observation of a given environment, while surveillance implies an ongoing observation [4]. It is certainly true that any of the tools and methods that we have discussed for conducting reconnaissance could be used in an ongoing manner as surveillance tools, and indeed some of them are, though extended operation of such tools would result in a very high likelihood of being discovered. Some of the same general techniques are still useful, but can be adapted to more long term eavesdropping on communications of voice and data, or emissions into the electromagnetic spectrum.

There is also the consideration that the target of surveillance may be internal to our nation or organization. Such cases are certainly more common in recent years, largely as a result of several large terrorist attacks having taken place. In the face of such activities, governments can often make a case, sometimes without consulting the public in the matter, for ongoing surveillance. Such programs are often implemented in the name of combating terrorism, drug trafficking, and other similar situations. Although there are also commonly laws that regulate domestic surveillance, such laws are not always followed to the letter, and in fact, are sometimes ignored entirely, in the name of the public good. We will discuss some of these issues in greater depth later in this section.

Voice Surveillance

On voice communication systems built on older analog technologies, conducting voice surveillance was literally a matter of wiring a device into the phone line at some point, called a wiretap. As we move forward into newer systems, such tasks become increasingly easier to carry out and easier to execute from a distance as well, but we continue to use the same term. In digital phone systems, such surveillance may be as easy as activating a feature in the systems controlling the voice traffic for a particular location, rendering a once manual task into a few clicks in an administrative tool.

WARNING

Conducting surveillance is fairly universally regulated by one or more wiretap laws in most countries around the globe. In the majority of cases, conducting surveillance without following very specific rules, even on privately owned systems may very well violate such laws and result in stiff penalties. In cases where such surveillance is required, consulting legal advice beforehand is strongly advised.

In recent years, Voice over IP (VoIP) traffic has begun to make large inroads toward replacing the Plain old Telephone service (POTs) as the standard for voice-based communications. For those that intend to conduct surveillance on such communications, this is actually a good thing, as VoIP traffic is considerably easier to eavesdrop on from a distance, and, depending on the implementation may have considerably less inherent security.

In essence, eavesdropping on unencrypted VoIP conversations, which may include many commercial and consumer services, is just a matter of having access to the network traffic in order to apply a sniffing device. Both sides of a voice conversation can be recorded in this manner, and can easily be decoded and played back using a tool such as Wireshark or Cain and Abel, both of which have a simple point and click interface which will play back an audio version of the conversation in a given packet capture file.

Data Surveillance

Data surveillance is a longer term, and often more pervasive, version of some of the tools and techniques that we have discussed in the reconnaissance sections of this chapter and Chapter 4. Data surveillance is often conducted by monitoring infrastructure devices that have been permanently or semi-permanently installed with the express purpose of listening to the traffic going over the network or networks in question.

In smaller scale installations, such as those that we might find in a corporation wishing to conduct such surveillance, this is often carried out though the installation of specialized surveillance devices, such as those produced by NIKSUN, at key areas in the network infrastructure. Such devices can allow traffic to be captured as it goes over the network in order to allow for later analysis of attacks, application usage, communications, and any number of network-oriented activities. While such solutions work very well for small to medium scale monitoring, they do not scale well when we wish to monitor much larger sets of data, such as monitoring of traffic or traffic patterns for an entire nation. For such purposes, the organizations, generally governments, that wish to do so generally implement their own solutions or have solutions custom built for them. Expect to see more activity in this area as more organizations move to the cloud.

Large Scale Surveillance Programs

The US government provides us with several good examples of government-scale surveillance systems. One of the earlier such attempts at enabling voice and data surveillance on a large scale was seen in Echelon. Echelon is the popular term used to refer to the network of signals intelligence collection and analysis operated by the parties to the US-UK Security Agreement, namely the United States, Canada, United Kingdom, Australia, and New Zealand. Echelon is large scale eavesdropping on international voice traffic over satellite, phone networks, microwave links, and even data sources such as fax transmissions and email. The original intent of Echelon was to monitor the communications of the Soviet Union and the countries allied with it in the 1960s. At present, it is believed to be used for monitoring of activities more along the lines of terrorism and drug trafficking, as well as to collect general intelligence information.

The Carnivore program was implemented by the US Federal Bureau of Investigation (FBI) in the late 1990s. Carnivore was a device that when attached at the Internet Service Provider (ISP) of the target intended to be monitored could filter out and record all traffic going to and from the target. Carnivore was not contextually aware, and could only filter traffic by the sending and receiving destinations [5]. After much public controversy, the Carnivore program was abandoned in 2001, and commercial replacements were put in place [6].

Another attempt at large scale data monitoring, once more from the FBI, was Magic Lantern, first publically disclosed in 2001 [7]. Magic Lantern worked on a somewhat different principle. The tactic for this application was to implement keystroke logging on a remote machine through the use of a Trojan horse or exploit delivered via e-mail [8]. Once the target had successfully executed the e-mail attachment bearing Magic Lantern, it would install and presumably begin to send logged data to a monitoring station. In 2002, the FBI confirmed the existence of Magic Lantern, but stated that it had never been deployed [9].

Einstein is a current and government-oriented data surveillance program. It began in 2002 as a program to monitor the network gateways of the US government for unauthorized traffic and intrusions [10]. Through several revisions it became a wider reaching program until in 2008, its use became mandatory for federal agencies, with the exception of the Department of Defense (DoD) and certain intelligence agencies. Although intended primarily as a measure to protect the systems of the US government, Einstein also collects a non-trivial amount of data as it reverses these networks [10]. The main goal of Einstein is "to identify and characterize malicious network traffic to enhance cyber security analysis, situational awareness, and security response [11]."

Perfect Citizen is an NSA program, designed to detect vulnerabilities in both public and privately run critical infrastructure systems and networks [12]. Although not a mandatory program, significant incentives in the form of government contracts have been offered to those that are willing to participate. Concerns have been raised over government entry into monitoring of private companies, such as utility companies.

Uses of Surveillance Data

Aside from the direct uses of surveillance data, we can also, given a sufficient amount of data, use it as a basis for detecting patterns of behavior among those being surveilled. The US government, and likely other governments as well, have been searching for exactly such patterns in voice and data communications for some time.

Since the terrorist attacks that took place on September 11, 2001, the US government, more specifically the National Security Agency (NSA), has been conducting pattern analysis on voice conversations in order to detect the patterns that might presage a terrorist attack [13]. Using such techniques, we can infer that certain patterns of voice traffic, for example, a call from a known terrorist friendly country to a location in the United States, then sequential calls from the number in the United States to six other numbers, may very well be an indicator of unusual activity. Of course, this assumes foreknowledge of which phone numbers to watch for such patters occurring, or an extremely powerful computing capability, likely beyond what currently exists.

COMPUTER NETWORK ATTACK

Computer Network Attack (CNA) is a military term defined as "Actions taken through the use of computer networks to disrupt, deny, degrade, or destroy information resident in computers and computer networks, or the computers and networks themselves [1]." While this term meshes well with the common viewpoint of basements full of hackers bringing cyber war to the enemy, or individual attackers conducting similar activities, we need to understand that there is a large difference in such activities conducted by nation states and non-nation states.

It is entirely true that, in a purely cyber war sense, small groups or individual attackers can potentially wield similar weapons to a similar level of effectiveness as a nation state, but the similarity will often end there. An individual hacker with access to the command and control system of a large botnet can certainly wreak havoc, but the capability to take the attack into conventional warfare, or to use the cyber attack as an accompaniment or compliment to other attacks is often reserved for those with much greater resources.

Another common confusion when discussing CNA is differentiating it from the attacks that we commonly see in the normal daily attacks from blackhat hackers, cyber criminals, and other similar groups that are not being actively sponsored by a nation state, or even in the attacks that we carry out against ourselves in the penetration testing process. The difference, primarily, is a matter of scope—intent—sponsorship, and completeness of the attack process.

Attacks conducted in the name of penetration testing and by random hackers do not usually "go for the throat" as we might in a conventional attack. Many such attackers work to compromise the target environment in order to own it, but do not take the destructive steps beyond that which might be required or desired in actual warfare. In genuine cyber warfare, where we have a presumably greater intent to significantly impact our target, such steps might lead to the wholesale destruction or disabling of critical infrastructure through a purely cyber attack, or might be used to disable systems that provide protection against a conventional attack, such as missile tracking systems, in order to facilitate such an attack.

Waging War in the Cyber Era

Cyber warfare capabilities are not only relatively new, when discussing them on their own merits, but they change the way conventional warfare is carried out as well. When we look at any of the current methods of warfare, cyber capabilities add new dimensions to them. In cyber warfare, we must consider the physical, electronic, and logical elements of warfare as major factors, as well as the reasons for our actions and the factor of time.

Physical Warfare

Cyber warfare can have great impact on the way physical war is waged. Given that even strictly physical warfare, in the sense of boots on the ground, depends a great deal on technologies, these things are vulnerable to cyber attack. Support for physical operations depends on supplies being delivered properly, soldiers being moved from one place to another on a tight schedule, communications functioning, and any number of other factors. If one or more of these activities does not take place, or, worse yet, is intentionally altered in order to engineer a weakness, our solely physical warfare can quickly degenerate into chaos.

On the other side of the coin, cyber warfare activities are very vulnerable to physical effects. If communications lines are severed, power is unavailable, environmental conditions cannot be maintained, or any of a number of other conditions cannot be met, our relatively fragile computer systems and infrastructure become so much dead weight.

In either case, physical warfare can affect or be affected by cyber warfare attacks. When the physical component is ignored in cyber warfare, we potentially lose a large portion of the entire picture. Cyber warfare is indeed a distinct dimension of warfare, but isolating it from the other dimensions renders its capabilities incomplete, at best.

Electronic Warfare

Although often considered a subset of conventional or physical warfare, electronic warfare can have a profound effect on cyber warfare and vice versa. Electronic warfare is largely concerned with attacks that take place in the electromagnetic spectrum (think analog vs digital), an area which the systems that are used to carry out cyber warfare make great use of, and from which they are very sensitive to interference. Using the tactics of electronic warfare, we can potentially render useless the systems and infrastructure that make up the cyber warfare capabilities of our opponents without landing a single physical blow.

Likewise, the systems that allow electronic warfare to be carried out are generally of a highly technological nature and are potentially susceptible to attack on a cyber level. One can envision an exchange where a nation-state would attempt to remove the cyber capability from an opponent via electronic warfare attack, only to find that its electronic warfare capability had been nullified by a cyber attack.

Logical Warfare

Of course, as we discussed in the beginning of this section, we also have strictly cyber oriented attacks to consider. Such attacks can be used for reconnaissance and surveillance, as we discussed earlier in this chapter, but they can also be used to conduct outright attacks against other systems and infrastructure. Such attacks are the meat of CNA and we will spend a considerable amount of time discussing them in the Attacks section, later in this chapter.

Purely logical attacks in isolation are very much lacking in their potential to be effective in an overall war effort. While it is very easy for nearly any party to obtain and utilize such weapons to great effect, not being able to follow up with other attacks is extremely limiting. If we consider conflicts of a conventional nature as an example, using cyber warfare tactics in isolation might be the equivalent of conducting conventional warfare without the use of air support; definitely possible, but very limiting.

Reactive vs Proactive Attacks

In considering cyber warfare attacks, we can act reactively, in the sense of defending against an attack or responding to the actions of our opponents. We can also act proactively, in the sense of anticipating activities stemming from threats or courses of action on the part of our opponents that would seem to indicate progress toward an undesirable state. Given cyber capabilities, we have the possibility of using tactics that are not immediately physical or overtly harmful, and do not require physical movement of troops or resources to carry out such activities.

When responding reactively, we will likely continue in the paradigm of traditional warfare. Although we do not necessarily need to move resources into the area, we still need to conduct many of the staging operations that are required to ramp up for such a conflict. In all likelihood, this will include conducting many of the reconnaissance activities that we discussed earlier in this chapter when we covered Computer Network Exploit (CNE), and may be able to benefit from any ongoing surveillance that was already in place against our target. Once such activities are completed to the extent that we have sufficient information to conduct attacks, we can then move on to CNA.

If we are to conduct cyber warfare proactively, we have a very large spectrum of warfare options that are open for use, up to and including an all-out attack. Of great potential usefulness, however, are attacks that are put in place in advance, but not triggered until conditions are the most appropriate and advantageous for us to do so. Such logic bomb tactics can be staged years in advance, and may even be insinuated into the systems of our opponent at a hardware level. We discussed such activities in greater depth in the Supply Chain Concerns section of Chapter 6. In such situations, carefully planned proactive activity can be used to render the opponent entirely impotent at the exact time in which they are most dependent on their tools and weapons to function properly.

The Attack Process

The attack process is usually focused on a particular system, or set of systems. In this process, as shown in Figure 5.1, we will likely conduct additional and more detailed reconnaissance and scanning, oriented toward gaining yet more specific information from the system. At this level, we can potentially conduct reconnaissance in greater

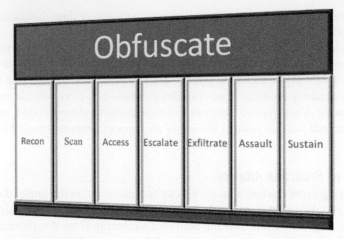

FIGURE 5.1 Attack Process

depth, as our need for secrecy and stealth may not be as great as it was while we were conducting CNE. We will then attempt to access the system, either through the use of an outright attack or using credentials that we have managed to gather from somewhere in the environment, through social engineering, or other means. Once we have an account on the system, we may need to escalate the level of access that we have in order to accomplish our goals. The target for such privilege escalation is often root or administrator level access, giving us relative freedom on the system. Given the needed level of access to the system, we can then exfiltrate any information that we wish to, cause damage to the environment in any way that benefits us, then install any measures that we need to in order to ensure future access.

Throughout the entire attack process, the attacker will also seek to cover or obfuscate their activities. They may want to appear to be attacking from a different location than where they are physically located, or take other steps to ensure that their attacks are not traced back to them. The attacker will also likely wish to remove any traces of their activities on the system when they leave it. This destruction of logs or forensic evidence can leverage lessons being learned in the hacker and cyber crime activities today.

Recon

We spent a good deal of time discussing reconnaissance and surveillance earlier in this chapter in the context of CNE. In that case, the reconnaissance that we would conduct would be done in a general sense, in order to map out and discover information on our target environment. As reconnaissance done in the context of CNA and of the attack process, we will likely already have such general information already from the CNE phase and will be hunting for information on a much more specific level, given our potentially greater level of access and reduced need for stealth.

Another tool that may become useful during this more specific stage of reconnaissance is social engineering. Using some of the social engineering tactics that we will cover in Chapter 6, we may very well be able to gain specific information that will allow us to access the systems in question without needing to resort to the full spectrum of attacks that we might need otherwise. Through social engineering we may be able to discover shared passwords used in other services or applications, may be able to find account names through searching the physical surroundings of those that work in the environment or through dumpster diving, or any number of similar tactics.

Given the task of long term reconnaissance at a more specific level, we may also want to plant the tools that would allow such monitoring on a particular system. Even on this scale, software such as a keystroke logger can produce enormous amounts of information, only a very small portion of which will generally have any great value; however, it may still be worth the effort. In environments where good password hygiene is not strictly enforced with technical controls, we can often find passwords that are manually synchronized between multiple systems, a great boon when attempting to gain access. We may also be able to sniff credentials from network traffic if less secure protocols such as telnet, File Transfer Protocol (FTP), or Post Office Protocol (POP) are allowed in the environment. The overall task of reconnaissance may involve a wide variety of tools and techniques, and will likely change heavily depending on the environment in question.

Scan

During the scanning portion of CNA, instead of the general port scans, fingerprinting, service versioning, and so on that we performed in our general reconnaissance, we will likely be much more closely examining the system for potential vulnerabilities during reconnaissance in CNA. In general, we will be scanning for further detailed information from applications, and potentially more specific information from the operating system itself.

When attempting to collect more information from applications, beyond cursory checks for programs and their versions, we will often focus on finding an exposed application that might be particularly talkative, such as a web interface to a database, and drilling down from there. This is often a manual process and can be time consuming, but can be very useful. We can often discover very specific information in this manner, such as database versions from error messages, potential usernames from conducting SQL injection attacks through the web interface, and any number of other bits and pieces of information.

NOTE

Not only can applications provide us an opportunity to surveil a remote system, but they can also potentially provide us an open doorway into the operating system itself. Improperly secured web applications are one of the main problem areas that allow such attacks to take place.

We may also want to collect additional information regarding the operating system such as specific patching information, uptime, or any of a number of other items that could potentially allow us to gain information through inference. Such additional small details may aid us in our attacks when we get to the attack and escalation steps of our process. As we discussed in the more general information collection sections of the first section of this chapter, documenting this information carefully can be very helpful through the entire process.

Access

Gaining access to a system can take place using a variety of tools and methods. If we have been successful in any of our previous attempts at social engineering, dumpster diving, stealing or cloning access card such as Common Access Cards (CACs), or have managed to find accounts with synchronized passwords on other systems that we have been able to access, we may very well have legitimate credentials with which we can simply log in. Slightly more complicated than this, although more likely, is that we will be able to find usernames that exist on the system and either crack or guess passwords, using some of the tools that we discussed in Chapter 4, in order to access them.

Another potential path that may gain us easy access would be to use client-side attacks against individual systems that belong to the users of our target system. Such attacks utilize vulnerabilities in software running on the client, such as a web browser, as an attack vector. We stand a much greater chance of being able to access individual workstations in order to gain access to credentials than we do when attempting to do access a server that is carefully maintained and patched. Client-side attacks can be web-based, use email as a delivery method, ride in on a USB drive, or any of a number of other methods. Particularly in non-technical working environments, such attacks enjoy a high degree of success, although we may not find as much success in highly secured environments.

We can also attempt to use common operating system or application exploits in order to access a system. We have likely, at some point in the process, already used one or more of a variety of vulnerability scanning tools, either during the more general reconnaissance process, or during the more specific examination during the attack process.

Escalate

Once we have gained some sort of access to a given system, we may need to gain additional or higher level privileges than those that we presently have, commonly known as privilege escalation. When we are attempting to gain access to accounts that have a higher level of privilege than those that we presently have, this is known as vertical privilege escalation. When we are attempting to gain access to different accounts that what we have access to, but are at the same level as the account that we already have access to, this is known as horizontal privilege escalation.

Privilege escalation of either variety can be accomplished through a variety of methods. We may be able to use a different set of exploits than we used previously, as we now have access to the system as a user. We may also be able to take advantage of misconfigurations or insecurely set configurations. It is entirely possible that, on some systems, the standard user account that we have managed to access may have the ability to act as an administrator directly, or may be able to escalate their privilege level as normal functionality of the operating system.

We may also be able to utilize the privileges of applications that are operating with heightened permissions. Applications such as those that run backups, various servers or daemons, or other processes that require privileges that are higher than the level of a general user are often vulnerable to attack. Various application flaws such as buffer overflows or race conditions can allow us to execute arbitrary code through these already running applications. We may also be able to access and modify interpreted scripts or shell scripts that are not secured properly, in order to pass operating system commands through them or gain direct access to an operating system shell.

Exfiltrate

Once we have gained the needed access to the environment, one of our primary concerns is to find any data that may be valuable to us, and exfiltrate it to a location that is accessible to us from another location, or to move it directly to our own systems. Exfiltration, in terms of Confidentiality, Integrity, and Availability (CIA), is an attack primarily against confidentiality, and potentially against availability.

We have a very wide variety of tools that we can use to exfiltrate data, from purpose-built tools and protocols that exist for the specific purpose of moving data around, to more general tools that can be bent to such a purpose, to out of band methods that might allow us to subvert security measures designed to specifically prevent such efforts.

In simple cases, we may be able to easily use common applications and protocols to move our files or data. File transfers can be accomplished with FTP, Secure Copy Protocol (SCP), Extensible Messaging and Presence Protocol (XMPP), or any of a number of other common protocols. In many environments we may find these particular transfer protocols blocked as outgoing traffic, but we will often find Hypertext Transfer Protocol (HTTP) traffic allowed, which will suit our purposes nicely. It is a rare and highly secure environment indeed where we will not be able to find some sort of outgoing protocol on which we can piggyback information.

Assault

The assault phase is what often makes it a military operation as it is a step typically not included in the penetration testing process, which, in general, closely mirrors our attack process. In the case of actual cyber warfare, it is likely that once we have managed to gain access to a machine, escalate to the privilege level that we need, and exfiltrate any interesting data we may want to use the system to sow chaos in the environment. In military terms, we have the five Ds to describe the effect of such activities: deception, disruption, denial, degradation, and destruction [14], as shown in Figure 5.2. In a CIA sense, these attacks will mainly be against availability and integrity.

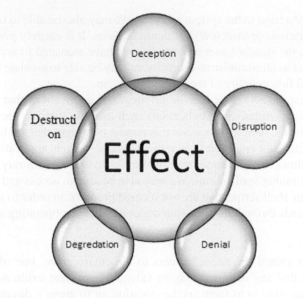

FIGURE 5.2 Five Ds

Sustain

Once we have gained sufficient access to a system, we may wish to reconfigure it to ensure our future ability to access it again. While we may have used a specific exploit to gain access to the system and escalate our privileges when we were first able to do so, we may not be able to count on the same points of entry being available in the future. Against this eventuality, we will likely want to secure additional access by creating new accounts, opening services on additional ports, installing command and control software, placing backdoors in applications, and so on.

The most successful such efforts will likely be those that are the least obvious and the least prone to being accidentally discovered by a system administrator. Some of the more blatant methods, such as opening a new listening port on the system may very well be found in short order, particularly on an internet-facing system. Additionally, we may want to be careful of leaving behind such measures in places where they might be found by another attacker. Many of the pre-built backdoors that are available will use a standard port by default, which could render our backdoor very easily located if we do not change it.

Obfuscate

Our likely first and last step on a system that we have compromised or intend to compromise is obfuscating. Obfuscate means "to confuse, bewilder, or stupefy [15]." We use this term to cover not only the methods that we might use to cover up or erase evidence of our intrusion, but also to potentially point any potential investigators to another source entirely. Obfuscation is really a layer that runs under all of the activities that we will take in the attack process. Some such obfuscatory actions take place even before our first recon, some take place during our various attacks, and some take place as our very last step before permanently vacating the system in question.

The simplest and earliest obfuscation measures that we might take are those that will prevent our attacks from being traced back to our actual physical location. Such tools might be various proxies, such as Tor, or intervening machines that we use as an intermediary connection before attacking, IP spoofing, or any of a number of other methods that we might use to disguise our point of origination. While some such tools may not be perfect in nature, they do provide an additional layer of protection in case our activities in the target environment are noticed.

We will also likely take steps to ensure that we do not leave digital forensic evidence behind on the target system. In such cases, we might change timestamps so that they reflect the original time before we modified any files, clean up any tools that we have moved to the system, remove or alter log entries, and generally ensure that we have not accidentally left any traces behind. On the other side of this same process, we may very well want to intentionally leave such traces behind but alter them so that they point to another source. If we can falsely attribute an attack to another source, this may not only cover our tracks, but cause significant confusion and consternation as well.

SUMMARY

In this chapter, we discussed the basics of Computer Network Exploitation (CNE). As we covered, CNE is a military term that does not use the term exploit in the way that it is typically used in the information security community, but instead uses it in the sense of exploiting data that we have gained through reconnaissance or surveillance to our own good.

We also discussed Computer Network Attack (CNA). We covered the different factors involved in cyber warfare, including the physical, logical, and electronic elements of warfare. We also covered reactive and proactive actions in warfare, and how these prompt a rather different set of actions in cyber warfare. These processes and the tools that we have discussed outline some of the major strategies and tactics that are used to conduct CNE and CNA. These tools are not unique, nor are many of them difficult to access, and the process can be simple, but to carry out cyber operations at the level of warfare for a nation-state requires a great deal of more resources, effort, and knowledge.

REFERENCES

[1] What are Information Operations. *Cyberspace and Information Operations Study Center.* [Online] July 24, 2010. [Cited: May 28, 2012.] <http://www.au.af.mil/info-ops/what. htm>.

[2] Leong, Patrick. Ethernet 10/100/1000 Copper Taps, Passive or Active? *lovemytool. com.* [Online] October 18, 2007. [Cited: May 28, 2012.] <http://www.lovemytool.com/ blog/2007/10/copper-tap.html>.

[3] Olzak, Tom. Protect your network against fiber hacks. *IT Security.* [Online] May 3, 2007. [Cited: May 28, 2012.] <http://blogs.techrepublic.com.com/security/?p=222&tag=nl. e036>.

[4] U.S. Marine Corps. Imagery Intelligence. s.l.: U.S. Marine Corps, 2002. MCWP 2–15.4.

[5] Tschabitscher, Heinz. How Carnivore Email Surveillance Worked. *About.com.* [Online] 2010. [Cited: May 28, 2012.] <http://email.about.com/od/staysecureandprivate/a/ carnivore.htm>.

[6] Associated Press. FBI Ditches Carnivore Surveillance System. *FoxNews.com.* [Online] January 18, 2005. [Cited: May 28, 2012.] <http://www.foxnews.com/ story/0,2933,144809,00.html>.

[7] Bradner, Scott. The FBI as an ethical hacker?. *Network World.* [Online] April 21, 2009. [Cited: May 28, 2012.] <http://www.networkworld.com/columnists/2009/042309bradner. html>.

[8] Sposato, Ike. The FBI's Magic Lantern. *WorldNetDaily.* [Online] November 28, 2001. [Cited: May 28, 2012.] <http://www.wnd.com/news/article.asp?ARTICLE_ID=25471>.

[9] Hentoff, Nat. The FBI's Magic Lantern. *The Village Voice.* [Online] May 28, 2002. [Cited: May 28, 2012.] <http://www.villagevoice.com/2002-05-28/news/the-fbi-s- magic-lantern/>.

[10] Department of Homeland Security Department of Homeland Security United States Computer Emergency Readiness Team. *Privacy Impact Assessment EINSTEIN Program.* s.l.: Department of Homeland Security Department of Homeland Security United States Computer Emergency Readiness Team, 2004. <http://www.dhs.gov/xlibrary/assets/ privacy/privacy_pia_eisntein.pdf>.

[11] (US-CERT), United States Computer Emergency Readiness Team. Privacy Impact Assessment for the Initiative Three Exercise. s.l.: Department of Homeland Security, 2010.

[12] Gorman, Siobhan. U.S. Plans Cyber Shield for Utilities, Companies. *The Wall Street Journal.* [Online] July 8, 2010. [Cited: May 28, 2012.] <http://online.wsj.com/article/ SB10001424052748704545004575352983850463108.html>.

[13] Singel, Ryan. Top Secret: We're Wiretapping You. *Wired.com.* [Online] March 05, 2007. [Cited: May 28, 2012.] <http://www.wired.com/science/discoveries/news/2007/03/7281 1?currentPage=all>.

[14] US Air Force. *Air Force Basic Doctrine.* s.l.: US Air Force, 1997. <http://www. globalsecurity.org/military/library/policy/usaf/afdd/afdd1.pdf>. Air Force Doctrine Document 1.

[15] Dictionary.com. Obfuscate. *Dictionary.com.* [Online] 2010. [Cited: May 28, 2012.] <http://dictionary.reference.com/browse/obfuscate>.

Psychological Weapons

INFORMATION IN THIS CHAPTER:

- Social Engineering Explained
- How the Military Approaches Social Engineering
- How the Military Defends Against Social Engineering

We talked about technical attacks in chapters four and five, now we will focus on using the target's behaviors to gain access to their information. Psychological Operations (PSY OPS) are planned operations to convey selected information and indicators to foreign audiences to influence their emotions, motives, objective reasoning, and ultimately the behavior of foreign governments, organizations, groups, and individuals [1]. Militaries have been conducting PSY OPS, or influence operations, for centuries. The United States stood up Army Special Forces (Green Berets') to win the hearts and minds rather than just force to achieve victory. Comparable techniques are used by Human Intelligence (HUMINT) collectors and the Intelligence community to get enemy personnel to betray their countries by becoming spies. Similar techniques have been used in civilian society by con artists whose ability to gain someone's trust so they can take advantage of them. Many of the methods are used by salespeople to influence buyers to purchase the most expensive car. Now these techniques are being modified by hackers and cyber warriors to get users to violate policies and common sense thus allowing them access to critical data—and are commonly referred to as Social Engineering.

SOCIAL ENGINEERING EXPLAINED

Social Engineering (SE) is the act of influencing someone's behavior through manipulating their emotions, or gaining and betraying their trust to gaining access to their system. This can be done in person, over the phone, via an email, through social media or a variety of other methods. The difference between social engineering and other attacks is the vectors are through the person, or as hackers say the "wetware" rather than the hardware.

The goal of an SE attack is to create a relationship, gain the targets trust, and get them to take an action or provide some information that is a violation of their organizations' policies or personal basic security practices. Some folks have the gift of gab and can do it with a cold call but most attackers will take time to prepare a story based on information known about the target. This attack vector has grown rapidly in the past few years and for some targets is the dominant technique.

Is Social Engineering science?

How is social engineering a science? There have been many recent publications on kinesics (the study of body and facial expressions) like Paul Ekman's books on micro facial expressions or 'What Every Body Is Saying: An Ex-FBI Agent's Guide to Speed—Reading People' by Marvin Karlins and Joe Navarro. These, combined with books on subjects like "Emotional Intelligence: Why It Can Matter More Than IQ" by Daniel Goleman and "Blink: The Power of Thinking Without Thinking" by Malcolm Gladwell, that talks about how intuition is based on insights the person may not be consciously aware of, start to develop a body of knowledge that can be applied as a science rather than an art. These studies are developing the baseline to take this discipline from an art to a science.

This leads to the question "can SE be taught, or is it a natural ability?" There is some debate on whether SE skills can be taught, but this is basically the same debate that exists for leadership, salesmanship, or any of a number of other such skills. Though the arguments are often very passionate, most will agree in the end that some people have natural tendencies that make them great when they study and train in the discipline they want to master while others can go through the same process and only become average. So while some individuals will naturally become very proficient at technical hacking they may struggle to use social engineering techniques like the "cold call" but everyone can learn the basics and find where their talents lay. Many of the tactics techniques and procedures we will discuss are a blend of technical and SE attacks.

SE Tactics Techniques and Procedures (TTPs)

A typical SE exploit depends on the target. There are two general scenarios: general access attacks and specific targeted access attacks. To use a metaphor (understanding most metaphors when applied to cyberspace are dangerous as they don't reflect the complexity of the environment), if we were ordered to steal a car in the next week that would be easy. In a general access attack, we could sit outside a convenience store waiting for someone to leave their car running then jump in and drive away (remember to check for a baby seat) or we could use a gun and car jack someone at a light, we could go old school and learn to hotwire a car or any number of other techniques. If we were told to steal the Commanding Generals car (a specific target), that would be a different story. In the first scenario we didn't need to do any reconnaissance, now we need to put a lot of effort into recon. We have to learn what they drive and figure out the best attack. We need to understand which attack has the least chance of getting caught, as the mayor controls the police force. Depending on our motivations we may want the theft to go unnoticed for a period of time, or we may want it to be dramatic so it gets on the evening news. The same rule is true with cyber attacks but as there is an element of personal interaction in SE it is even more relevant to understand the target.

First let's look at general attacks. These are attacks where the goal is to gain entry to any system or network. The attacker is indifferent to the owner of the system. A general phishing attack would be a good example (see note for definitions on types). The cost of sending out the emails is low, there are about 183 billion spam emails sent a day and 2.3% are phishing attacks [2]. These systems can be attacked or used to attack other systems (making them "zombies"). Harvesting large number of systems is useful to build systems in between the attacker and the targets. There is NO need for reconnaissance as the attacker doesn't care where the system is or what is does, they can move directly to the attack phase and due to the low costs accept the lower number of compromised systems. So to build a botnet army this would be a great SE-based technique.

The next example of a general attack is to release a targeted virus (i.e. only attacks specific notations military systems). A virus is a malcode program that the user needs to run to have it work. Attackers can load a virus into a word doc, PDF, power point, picture, or even a game. These infected files will open and run (i.e. someone can open the power point and go through the slides) at the same time the virus infects the system. The down side to an attack like this is it can go viral and end up infecting systems it was not intended to attack. This kind of an attack can also be done with a worm which is a malcode program that doesn't need user interaction, it will infect a system and use it to infect others but this would not be a SE attack, it would be categorized as a technical attack. The proliferation of translation sites on the web and ease of access to interesting news from the targets homeland have made this type of attack much easier. Developing believable scenarios with proper grammar and cultural context that will often get potential victims to take the bait.

NOTE

Standard types of attacks generally designed to steal identities:

- *Phishing:* This is where a mass email is sent to a large group of addresses (potentially millions). The email could try to lead the user to open an attachment or go to a web page, either of these actions would lead to the computer system being compromised (assuming the system in question was vulnerable).
- *Pharming:* Misdirecting users to a fraudulent Website.
- *Spear Phishing:* This is where a specific individual is targeted and a tailored email is sent that they will open and react to. Examples would be the Sys Admin for a network or Program Manager of a target. This requires collection of good intelligence on the intended target.
- *Whaling:* This is a Spear Phishing attack against the senior level of leadership of the organization being targeted.
- *Smishing:* SMS text designed to get user to go to compromised website or give up identity information.
- *Vishing:* Getting someone to call using Voice over IP (VoIP) to gain access to personal or financial data on the system during a call.

Now we will analyze target specific attacks. The attacker will approach the target after learning as much about them as they can via what the military calls Open Source Intelligence (OSINT). Civilians would just call this "googling" someone. The attacker wants to understand the victim's interests, fears, motivations, attitudes, and desires. This will allow the attacker to tailor the attack and increase the chances of success. Key information includes knowledge on significant dates (birth, marriage...), addresses, phone numbers, family members, interests, relationships, photographs, and work and education histories. If the target is active on social networking sites this is a great place to start; the greater their electronic footprint the better. There are many places to learn about the target:

- Personal info can be found on social media sites like Facebook or MySpace (this includes relationships, activities like sports, volunteering, religion practices, political beliefs...).
- Professional info is on networking sites like LinkedIn or job sites like Monster (this also tells you what they are working on).
- Geolocation info on sites like Google earth or location-based services like Foursquare.
- Financial info like tax records and homeownership records.
- What they are thinking can be read on via their twitters or blogs.
- Involvement in virtual worlds like Second Life or gaming site (where people can meet as any avatar they create).
- Membership info from organizations like academic alumni, clubs, professional organizations, or hobbies.

Types of SE approaches

Once the attacker has gathered the background information necessary to understand some options to approach the target they must decide how aggressive they want to be. From least to most aggressive the approaches are; observation, conversation, interview, interrogation, and torture. They can start by digital or physical observation. Next comes a conversation (electronic, telephonic, or in person). This is often the phase where the attacker will determine who they want to recruit or attack. Typically this is known as elicitation which is generally the extraction of information through what seems to be casual conversation. To phrase this another way it is where the con or story is based on the SE's ability to spin a lie. This ability comes from pretexting which is developing a scenario where the SE gains the trust of the person who owns or has access to the

---

TIP

Privacy has different meanings to individuals based on their generation and the culture they were raised in. Many of the younger generation have been raised with computers (sometimes called Digital Natives) live a large part of their lives online, to the point some have their diaries as part of their public web pages. Their expectations of privacy are different that most of the folks running the militaries and intelligence communities today. They can become vectors for attack if they have relationships with someone that has been targeted. It is important that both parties understand what is being posted and what is acceptable.

> **WARNING**
>
> The Financial Modernization Act of 1999 more commonly known as the Gramm-Leach-Bliley Act makes pretexting a crime. Under federal law it's illegal for anyone to [3]:
>
> - Use false, fictitious or fraudulent statements or documents to get customer information from a financial institution or directly from a customer of a financial institution.
> - Use forged, counterfeit, lost, or stolen documents to get customer information from a financial institution or directly from a customer of a financial institution.
> - Ask another person to get someone else's customer information using false, fictitious or fraudulent statements or using false, fictitious or fraudulent documents, or forged, counterfeit, lost, or stolen documents.
> - The Federal Trade Commission Act also generally prohibits pretexting for sensitive consumer information.

information in order to get them to break their policies or violate common sense and give the information to the attacker. One method that is used in every type of attack but is especially useful here is mirroring. For example by adopting the targets speech mannerism (or email style) it will be much easier to get them to engage in a conversation.

The next technique is to conduct an interview or outright interrogation. Both of these require the victim to submit to the attacker's authority. This can be done by posing as a customer who needs the information to make a decision, pretending to be someone from the government who has the right to the information, or through intimidation. These attacks can be done cold, or can be done after a relationship has been developed. The attacker can perform them in person using props like badges, or over the phone/email using spoofing to make it appear like the contact is from a legitimate source. An example would be to call someone on the Help Desk and tell them they have to reset the users account because of a mistake made during a recent update. Most people want to be helpful, and automatically trust their computer. That desire to help or trust in their system is the key to compromising them. Both of these techniques are not by their nature antagonistic. Often the most effective techniques are based on establishing common bonds. All of these techniques require building a relationship based on trust. Finally, for interrogation purposes, comes torture, but this is beyond SE practices. Figure 6.1 shows the flow of these techniques.

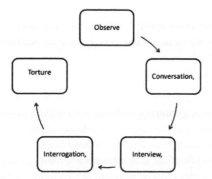

FIGURE 6.1 Approach Techniques From Most to Least Aggressive

Types of SE methodologies

Some typical methodologies for general collection are divided into physical and electronic. Physical techniques include things like: Dumpster Diving (digging though the targets trash), Shoulder Surfing (looking at their screen or keyboard while they work), Observation (tracking their activities—think stakeout), Spy Gear (like directional microphones / hidden cameras), and Impersonation (posing as utility worker). Electronic techniques include: Open web search (learn to use all the features of your search engine—i.e. Google will just search blogs), Pay for Service sites like Intelius or US Search, Credit Information Requests, Social networking site searches, Professional networking site searches, and geolocation sites (i.e. Google Street View).

Though this information is generally open the SE may need some tools to make the research more effective. These include web sites and tools like:

- American Registry for Internet Numbers (ARIN) (IP address information and Phone numbers for North America).
- Freedom of Information Act requests, OpenBook (Facebook searches).
- Maltego 3 (link mapping).
- Social Engineering Toolkit (technical hacks against the user).
- TwitScoop and Tweepz (twitter searches).
- Trendistic (tracks terms hot on twitter).
- TwitterMap (geolocation).
- PicFrog (image searches).
- TinyURL (allows URL redirection).
- Edgar [www.sec.gov/edgar] (corporate info).
- Sites like Spokeo (people search) and Telespoof.com (caller ID spoofing).

Then we have physical things like:

- Props (everything from clipboards to toolkits to deliveries).
- Fake business cards, disguises (facial features or uniforms), and fake or cloned badges.

This is just a short list of some of the different types of tools that can be employed as part of social engineering and the list is constantly evolving so search on comparisons to these tools as well.

One recent event that has captured the media's attention was the SE Capture the Flag event at DEFCON 18 called "How Strong Is Your Schmooze." There has always been a network based-CTF event but in 2010 there was a SE CTF. Here is an excerpt from the report on the event:

"Contestants were assigned a target company, with each having two weeks to use passive information gathering techniques to build a profile. No direct contact between the contestant and the target was allowed during this time. The information was compiled into a dossier that was turned in and graded as part of the contestant's score. During DefCon, contestants were then allowed 25 min to call their target and collect as many flags as possible, which made up the remainder of their score. Flags were picked to be non-sensitive information, and each was assigned

a point value based on the degree of difficulty in obtaining the information associated with the flag. A few examples of the 25 flags are: In House IT Support, New Hire Process, Anti-Virus Used, Is there a Cafeteria, Wireless On-Site, Badges for Bldg Access, and What OS Used.

Complex searches lead the contestants to gather quite a few PDFs or web pages that answered each of their inquires in full detail. One interesting surprise was the use of Google Street View as an information gathering tool. A primary factor in the success or failure of the contestant was the planning of the overall attack. The most interesting aspect of this has to do with how quickly and easily information could be obtained from all companies in a relatively short period of time, even with the caller under pressure. Final results were15 companies called and 14 of them had flags captured" [4].

During DEFCON 19 "The Schmooze Strikes Back" was held and a "Kids Edition" was added for 8–16 years old. DEFCON 20 will be called "Battle of the Sexes." This is one of the events to read the annual report from.

HOW THE MILITARY APPROACHES SOCIAL ENGINEERING

The military has been in the spy—counterspy business from the beginning, they are also experts at interrogation. Spying is the long con, whereas interrogation is generally the method used to get access to information in an immediate situation. This section will focus on the near term gathering of data (or the short con) as it applies directly to SE. We will look at the techniques used to extract information and discuss how they can be applied to SE.

First, we must understand that these techniques have been developed to work in both peacetime operations and combat situations. They are normally done in a controlled environment and are very similar to the techniques used by law enforcement agencies. The basic principles are similar to SE and the foundational principles as well as many of the techniques apply to SE attacks. The military trains and educates interrogators and most will stay in the discipline their entire careers. They become proficient in the languages and culture of their assigned region. Human Intelligence (HUMINT) operators or Interrogators are trained to deal with screening refugees, debriefing US and allied forces, interrogating prisoners of war, interview collaborators, exploiting captured material, liaising with host nation, acting as interpreters if needed, and interacting with the local population.

Army Doctrine

We will discuss how the Army deals with interrogation as they are the ones who are on the ground dealing with these issues. The basic techniques we will cover are from "FM 2-22.3 HUMAN INTELLIGENCE COLLECTOR OPERATIONS September 2006" [5].

Goal—collector's objective during this phase is to establish a relationship with the source that results in the source providing accurate and reliable information in response to the HUMINT collector's questions.

Key principles—From a psychological standpoint, the HUMINT collector must be cognizant of the following behaviors:

- Want to talk when they are under stress and respond to kindness and understanding during trying circumstances.
- Show deference when confronted by superior authority.
- Operate within a framework of personal and culturally derived values.
- Respond to physical and, more importantly, emotional self-interest.
- Fail to apply or remember lessons they may have been taught regarding security if confronted with a disorganized or strange situation.
- Be willing to discuss a topic about which the HUMINT collector demonstrates identical or related experience or knowledge.
- Appreciate flattery and exonerate them from guilt.
- Attach less importance to a topic if it is treated routinely by the HUMINT collector.
- Resent having someone or something they respect belittled, especially by someone they dislike.

These principles are used to develop an approach, build rapport, and establish a relationship in which the HUMINT collector presents a realistic persona designed to evoke cooperation from the source. In the military things are usually done in accordance with established procedures and if it is a mission (like an interrogation) it should have a documented plan. This is not to say they are not flexible and resist innovation but rather to say they want increase the chances of mission accomplishment and have found that having a plan to start with leads to greater success. The HUMINT collector must ensure their body language and personal representation match their approach.

Some standard operating approach techniques are: direct, incentive, emotional (Love / Hate / Fear / Pride / Futility / Anger), "we know all" or "file / dossier," rapid-fire (don't let them talk), Mutt and Jeff or good cop / bad cop, and false flag (misrepresentation of oneself). See figure 6.2 for how these relate to each other. The direct

FIGURE 6.2 The Various Approaches Must be Integrated

approach is simple and straightforward. It is simply telling the person what they want and using interview/interrogation skills to convince them to cooperate and share the information. This technique is useful in a conventional war but not very useful in counterinsurgencies or for social engineering. Statistics from interrogation operations in World War II show that the direct approach was effective 90% of the time. In Vietnam and in Operations URGENT FURY (Grenada, 1983), JUST CAUSE (Panama, 1989), and DESERT STORM (Kuwait and Iraq, 1991), the direct approach was 95% effective. The effectiveness of the direct approach in Operations ENDURING FREEDOM (Afghanistan, 2001–2002) and IRAQI FREEDOM (Iraq, 2003) are still being studied; however, unofficial studies indicate that in these operations, the direct approach has been dramatically less successful [5]. The military is still analyzing the reasons but one common assumption is that the motivations of religious fanaticism are harder to compromise than traditional nationalism.

There are some general types of direct questions that are useful: Initial (get the discussion going), Topical (focused on establishing how much they will communicate and what their level of knowledge is), Follow-up (making sure we have gained all the primary and peripheral information), Non-pertinent (establishing rapport and keeping discussion going), Repeat (seeing if they are consistent), Control (establish baseline), and Prepared (for areas interviewer is unfamiliar with or highly technical topics). One of the key questions here is the control or baseline question. It establishes how someone behaves when they are telling the truth. Much like a polygraph test starts with questions like your name and address then gradually builds to questions related to guilty actions so they can compare the stress reactions to the baseline a SE must understand how the target behaves when not under stress to judge reactions correctly.

The indirect approach, or using elicitation, can often be useful as we combine the information gathering with normal conversations with targets of interest without them knowing they are being interrogated. Elicitation is a sophisticated technique used when conventional collection techniques cannot be used effectively. Of all the collection methods, this one is the least obvious. However, it is important to note that elicitation is a planned, systematic process that requires careful preparation [6]. This is where the more the interviewer knows about the target the better, so they can have a natural flowing conversation. For example they may start by sharing information they have so the target assumes they know all about it and will openly discuss the details. This can be done in person or over social media.

Next comes incentive—this is basically offering the target something they want or need. The first thing that comes to mind is bribing them, but it can be as simple as an email offering to increase their speed or access to the internet. This approach can be very effective when tied to the right emotions. The emotional approach is where the targets emotions are brought into the interaction to get them to take an action that they would not normally do. A recent example of this is what is known as scareware. A good example would be when a pop-up box will announce there is a problem on the system that can be fixed by installing a free update. The update is a Trojan horse and doesn't do anything but compromise their system. This approach is based on

Fear, other emotions that can be used are: Love (in its many forms), Hate or Anger (us against them), Pride (in themselves or their organization), and Futility (there is no other option). Picking the right emotion is easier in person because we can read the body language or on the phone where we can judge the tone of voice and modify the approach based on the situation. The goal of this method is to manipulate the targets emotions so they override their natural cognitive reactions.

Other well known techniques are—"we know all" or "the file / dossier," this is where the interrogator would come in and lay a folder labeled "witness statements" or a DVD labeled "surveillance footage" on the desk. They would contain no actual information but allows the interrogator to start by saying something like "we have the evidence we need but want to get your side of the story before we submit our final report." For SE the presentation of material that supports the belief that we know the basic but just need them to provide the details. If they are still not talking freely it may be time to try the rapid-fire method where we keep interrupting them so they get frustrated and jump in with key facts so we will listen. It is also used when the target is going to say something that the interrogator doesn't want them to say like "I never went to that site" because once they tell a lie it is harder to get to the truth as first we must make them admit they lied.

The last two methods we will discuss are "Mutt and Jeff" or "Good cop / Bad cop," and false flag. We have all seen the aggressive and compassionate interview team in movies. The target will identify with the compassionate person and tell their story so they will shield them from the aggressive one. It can also be a really abusive interrogator follow by one who apologized for the unprofessionalness of their colleague. Typically the good cop would help the target rationalize their actions so they can talk about them openly. One way this method can be used by SE's is on social networking sites, we could present a Fakebook personality created for the attack as a cyber bully and a second as someone defending the target. Finally using the false flag, for the military this might be having a new interrogator come in and pretend to be from a friendly country or a non-government origination like the Red Cross. This is very useful as it is simply misrepresentation and is a bedrock of Social Engineering.

We can see that most of the techniques used by the military are directly applicable to the civilian sector and can be applied to both physical and cyber environments. The most important aspects the military brings are proven Tactics, Techniques, and Procedures (TTPs) and careful mission preparation and planning. These when applied to Social Engineering will give the attacker a strong capability to be successful on their mission.

HOW THE MILITARY DEFENDS AGAINST SOCIAL ENGINEERING

As the military approach to SE section discussed, the military has been in the spy—counterspy business from the beginning. The counterspy techniques are the same skills needed to defend against SE. Today's solider needs to understand counterintelligence (CI), counterterrorism, force protection, and Operational Security (OPSEC) techniques. This section will focus on the tactical level actions than can be done for CI. First let's review the doctrinal definitions for the key concepts:

- *Counterintelligence*—Information gathered and activities conducted to protect against espionage, other intelligence activities, sabotage, or assassinations conducted by or on behalf of foreign governments or elements thereof, foreign organizations, or foreign persons, or international terrorist activities [1].
- *Cyber Counterintelligence*—Measures to identify, penetrate, or neutralize foreign operations that use cyber means as the primary tradecraft methodology, as well as foreign intelligence service collection efforts that use traditional methods to gauge cyber capabilities and intentions [1].
- *Counterespionage*—That aspect of counterintelligence designed to detect, destroy, neutralize, exploit, or prevent espionage activities through identification, penetration, manipulation, deception, and repression of individuals, groups, or organizations conducting or suspected of conducting espionage activities [1].
- *Counterterrorism*—Actions taken directly against terrorist networks and indirectly to influence and render global and regional environments inhospitable to terrorist networks [1].
- *Force Protection*—Preventive measures taken to mitigate hostile actions against Department of Defense personnel (to include family members), resources, facilities, and critical information. Force protection does not include actions to defeat the enemy or protect against accidents, weather, or disease [1].
- *Operations Security (OPSEC)*—A process of identifying critical information and subsequently analyzing friendly actions attendant to military operations and other activities to: (a) identify those actions that can be observed by adversary intelligence systems; (b) determine indicators that adversary intelligence systems might obtain that could be interpreted or pieced together to derive critical information in time to be useful to adversaries; and (c) select and execute measures that eliminate or reduce to an acceptable level the vulnerabilities of friendly actions to adversary exploitation [1].

The military depends on confidentiality and secrecy. They deploy encryption, data classification, clearances for their personnel and a thorough set of processes and regulations. Soldier, Airmen, Seamen, and Marines understand the trust they have been given and the level of National Security compromise that could occur (not necessarily through a single loss of data but the aggregate knowledge impact as well). Cybersecurity has become a critical component of the National

FIGURE 6.3 Counterintelligence is a National Concern; This is the US Strategy to Deal with It [7]

Counterintelligence Strategy (see Figure 6.3). The mission to secure the nation against foreign espionage and electronic penetration of the IC, DoD, and to protect US economic advantage, trade secrets, and know-how is becoming a core responsibility for them.

CI has an offensive aspect as well. There is a need to set up traps or as they are called in cyberspace "honey pots" to attract insiders accessing information they are not authorized for. We need to have enticing files with embedded beacons that report back on where they are to see what has leaked out. We need to fund programs to gain access to the types of organizations that have the motives and means to attack the US and see what they have stolen. We need to conduct exercises and tests on our personnel to assess our readiness level. Finally we need to enforce consequences on individuals caught violating policies.

How the Army Does CI

Army Regulation (AR) 381-12 Threat Awareness and Reporting Program October 4, 2010 (for the old soldiers this was called Subversion and Espionage Directed against the US Army or SAEDA) establishes the training requirements and reporting procedures for counterintelligence. It also lays out indicators or suspicious activities like: foreign influence or connections, disregard for security practices, unusual work behavior, financial matters, foreign travel, undue interest, soliciting others, and extremist activity. This is basically a process that encourages every member of the staff to become a security officer and help police both themselves and their coworkers. The program is built around two key principles—situational awareness and behavior monitoring, both for themselves and the rest of the staff. Such a program done well can counter the whole spectrum of crime, internal threats (disgruntled or unstable workers), external threats (foreign operatives and terrorist), and today's Social Engineers. If done poorly it allows incidents like the recent unauthorized release of a large number of classified documents relating to the US war in Iraq to WikiLeaks. For the sake of brevity, we're not going to delve into the processes of the Navy and Marine Corps, although they're both quite capable in their own right at these processes and procedures.

An Air Force Approach

The Air Force Public Affairs Agency has published a "Social Media" Guide. Social media and the Air Force—Air Force Public Affairs Agency. Top 10 tips include items like: OPSEC is crucial to our mission, be aware of the image you present—the image you present will set the tone for your message and the enemy is engaged—you must engage there as well [7]. This is a very good example as it does a couple of things well. First the guide is more about what we should use rather than why we should not use the many different communication applications on the web. Second it is a formal policy that includes punitive consequences for misbehavior.

An important aspect of this defensive capability is to analyze the information that is leaking and conduct the appropriate investigation to determine what actions need to be taken. Historically there are examples like Aldrich Ames, Robert Hanssen, Colonel Vladimir Vetrov, a KGB defector known as the Farewell Dossier, Gregg Bergersen, and the eleven Russian spies recently deported from the US but these operations are time consuming, expensive and risky where we can get much of the same material through cyber spying. The risk of getting caught is lower, the time to gain access is faster, and the cost is cheaper. We have talked extensively about computer network exploitation, when we combine that with Social Engineering we have a paradigm shift in spying capabilities. This requires us to look at the techniques that got these traditional spies caught—careful analysis, auditing financial records, tips from co-workers, offensive operations to gain access to enemy files to see who they had turned into spies, and encouraging defectors to come over.

SUMMARY

Social Engineering (SE) is a very dangerous threat vector to all organizations and individuals. It requires training and vigilance to defend against. A simple questionnaire to someone asking them to answer questions so they can become closer friends could include the same questions asked to reset their password and how the organization is compromised. We need to make sure people are vigilant and cautious (remember we're not paranoid if they are out to get you). We can leverage lessons learned in the military to understand how these works and how we defend ourselves. Defenses against Social Engineering must be focused on behaviors.

The policies, culture, and training must be reinforced often to insure the workforce stays vigilant. Training the staff to have situational awareness is one of the keys to a good counter-SE program. This training must be continuous with messages from multiple sources—emails, meetings, and formal training. There need to be exercises to test the staff like emails asking employees to go to a site and enter their password only to find a message from the company that they would have allowed hackers to gain access to the network if it was a real attack. Security audits should include SE attacks to validate the training is effective. There is a saying in the hacker community—"You can't patch stupid," this often refers to the fact if a organization has a great technical security infrastructure and they can get through them, just go after the people. People are not stupid, they just don't understand the risks they are taking with their actions—training can fix that.

Bottom line—this is the growth area for threat vectors via social media and the only way to defend against it is executive awareness, user training, and validation exercises.

REFERENCES

[1] DoD. Joint electronic library [online, cited: May 28, 2012]. <http://www.dtic.mil/doctrine/>.
[2] Commtouch software Ltd Q1 2010 Internet threats trend report [online, cited: May 28, 2012]. <http://www.commtouch.com/download/1679>.
[3] 1999, Financial modernization act of. Federal trade commission. Facts for consumers [online, cited: May 28, 2012]. <http://www.ftc.gov/bcp/edu/pubs/consumer/credit/cre10.shtm>.
[4] Hadnagy CJ, Aharoni M, O'Gorman J. Defcon 18 social engineering CTF—how strong is your schmooze. socialengineer.org [online, cited: May 28, 2012]. <http://www.social-engineer.org/resources/sectf/Social-Engineer_CTF_Report.pdf>.

[5] Army, US FM 2-22.3 (FM 34-52) Human Intelligence Collector Operations. *Public affairs*; September 2006 [online]. <https://armypubs.us.army.mil/doctrine/DR_pubs/dr_aa/pdf/fm2_22x3.pdf>.

[6] Office of the director of national intelligence's office of the national counterintelligence executive [online, cited: May 28, 2012]. <http://www.ncix.gov/publications/policy/2008_Strategy.pdf>.

[7] Social media' guide. air force public affairs agency emerging technology division [online, cited: May 28, 2012]. <http://info.publicintelligence.net/USAFsocialmedia.pdf>.

Defensive Tactics and Procedures

INFORMATION IN THIS CHAPTER:

- What We Protect
- Security Awareness and Training
- Defending Against Cyber Attacks

Computer Network Defense (CND) is defined by the US Department of Defense (DoD) as "Actions taken through the use of computer networks to protect, monitor, analyze, detect, and respond to unauthorized activity within Department of Defense information systems and computer networks" [1]. The broad scope of these CND activities may very well include components that would be considered Computer Network Exploitation (CNE) and Computer Network Attack (CNA), as we discussed in Chapter 5. Additionally, the strategies and tactics developed and utilized in conducting CNE and CNA against our opponents can be used to strengthen our own defenses. CND is also one of the few places in Computer Network Operations (CNO) where we will find military and civilian approaches to be very similar.

In the military sense, CND may very well parallel the strategies and tactics that are used for conventional defense. The cyber equivalent of defensive emplacements, listening posts, patrols, and so on can be formulated, and the defensive strategies of conventional warfare can be adapted to cyber warfare by mapping the concepts across. Although this may not always be the most efficient means for us to use the tools of cyber warfare, it does allow time tested concepts to be applied to the new dimension of warfare. Given that the military leadership that is presently planning and carrying out CNE and CNA is likely to have been educated in the affairs of war before the advent of cyber warfare, this is the approach that we will most likely find in CND when executed by a nation state. This may also pose a possible weakness in CNO in general, as it does tend to add a certain element of inflexibility. Although it would be a gross generalization to call this a universal problem, we may find that some portion of military leadership will be hindered by conventional thinking on defense in the area of CND.

As we discussed in Chapter 5 when we talked about CNA, being able to execute the complete cycle of CND will more than likely require resources similar to those of a nation state. In a pure cyber attack sense, a non-nation state can certainly be capable of defending against an attack. In the attacks that occurred against the Chinese assets of Google in late 2009 and early 2010, we can see a good example of a large organization defending against attacks of a purely cyber nature. The attacks were focused on both disrupting the infrastructure of Google in China and on the theft of intellectual property through a variety of vectors.

Google's response to these attacks was to increase the level of hardening and redundancy in their infrastructure and architecture, and to ensure that patching and security applications were universally implemented and kept up to date [2]. In a pure cyber attack sense, such a response is completely acceptable and likely to be successful in most cases. In the complete form of CNA, as we discussed in the Waging War in the Cyber Era section of Chapter 5, we would likely see a nation state include elements of conventional warfare. Although a large entity, Google is not quite on the level of a nation state just yet, and is much less prepared to fend off an attack that included physical attacks as a component so would have to depend on the law enforcement and military of the nation where the attack was perpetrated.

WHAT WE PROTECT

When we look to defending against cyber attacks, it is often useful to examine what exactly it is that we are defending. In a very general sense, we are almost always concerned with the protection of information in one form or another.

Sensitive information, in the eye of the general public, is often categorized as Personally Identifiable Information (PII) or Patient Healthcare Information (PHI), and involves names, addresses, social security numbers, medical records, financial records, and a multitude of similar information. Such information, when compromised can lead to a variety of fraudulent activities, commonly gathered under the umbrella term of identity theft. Such activities can range from credit accounts being opened with stolen credentials to real estate being sold without the authorization of the legitimate owner, to simple theft of funds from bank accounts.

In the world of the military and government, information of a sensitive nature being exposed can have far greater consequences than mere financial loss. Information housed by such agencies can include Operations Orders (OPORDERS), war plans, troop movements, technical specifications for weapons or intelligence collection systems, identities of undercover intelligence agents, and any number of other items critical to the functioning of military and government. When such information is accessed in an unauthorized fashion, lives can be lost on a large scale and the balance of power can be shifted.

Laws do exist to protect these types of information, but they are, in many cases, still a work in progress. In the United States, as far as laws on data regarding individuals go, laws at this point are fairly weak on a federal level. Individual states have gradually begun to enact more stringent data protection and privacy laws, such as SB 1386 in California, in order to compensate for this weakness. Regarding the data held by governments, the military, and some industries, the custodians of such information generally have very strict laws and regulations regarding specifically how the information is handled and controlled, thus putting them in a much better position to protect the data for which they are responsible.

Confidentiality, Integrity, Availability (CIA)

The measures we take to protect our information assets can generally be described in terms of the classic CIA triad of confidentiality, integrity, and availability, as shown in Figure 7.1. The confidentiality of data refers to keeping it out of the hands of those that are not authorized to see it, the integrity of data refers to preventing unauthorized modifications to data or system functions, and the availability of data refers to being able to access it when needed. These basic principles govern how we go about securing the data with which we are concerned.

When protecting the confidentiality of data, we are concerned with keeping it out of the hands of those that do not have permission to access it. In terms of specific security implementations, this typically mean access controls and encryption in order to provide such protections. When applying these measures, we need to consider both data at rest and data in motion. Depending on where the data is at any given point in time, we may need to use different security controls, or different methods within a given control. We can see the results of lapses in confidentiality with the large breaches of PII that seem to occur with disturbing frequency in recent years, such as the loss of the US Department of Veterans Affairs (VA) laptop containing

FIGURE 7.1 CIA Triad

> **TIP**
>
> A less well-known alternative to the CIA triad, referred to as the Parkerian hexad, exists as well. The Parkerian hexad, developed by Donn Parker, breaks the same general concepts down into the categories of confidentiality, possession, integrity, authenticity, availability, and utility, allowing for a more detailed discussion of the relevant security concepts in a given situation [4]. The use of the Parkerian hexad allows us to be more specific when discussing security scenarios or situations without having to bend the rules of our model.

PII on US veterans in May of 2010. This was at least, the second breach of this type for the VA and cost them almost $13M, far more than the cost of implementing an encryption program [3].

When we look to protect the integrity of data, we are trying to prevent it from being manipulated in an unauthorized manner. Similarly to the measures that we use to provide confidentiality, we can use encryption to help provide integrity by making the data difficult to successfully manipulate without the proper authorization. In particular, hashes or message digests, such as MD5 and SHA1, are often used to ensure that messages or files have not been altered from the original by creating a fingerprint of the original data that can be tracked over time. Failures in integrity can have serious effects if we are not aware that they have happened, as data in the form of communications or files can be freely altered to reverse their meaning or to alter the outcome of decisions based on the data in question. When we think about the command and control systems used today it is easy to imagine the kind of havoc that could result in misinformation.

The availability of data simply means that we can access it when we need to do so. Ensuring availability means that we must be resilient in the face of attacks that might corrupt or delete our data or deny us access to it by attacking the environment in which it rests. It also means that we need to have a sufficiently robust environment in order to cope with system outages, communication problems, power issues, and any number of issues that might prevent us from accessing our data. Availability is often accomplished through the use of redundancy and backups for our data and for our environments. This is important to both weapon systems, critical infrastructure like the energy grid, and command and control systems.

Authenticate, Authorize, and Audit

Authentication, authorization, and auditing are commonly known as AAA; shown in Figure 7.2. These are the principles that allow us to practically carry out the securing of data. These are the means through which we can control and track how our data is being accessed, and by who, thus enabling us to enforce the policies that we have created to keep the data secure.

Authentication is the means by which we verify the identity of an individual or system against a presented set of credentials. A very common implementation of an authentication scheme is the combination of login and password. In this particular

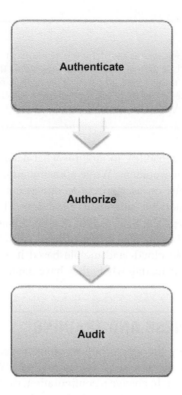

FIGURE 7.2 AAA

case, the user's login name is the identity presented, and it is verified against a stored form of the password that the user has given. A common implementation of authentication used by the US Department of Defense (DoD) is the Common Access Card (CAC). The CAC, sometimes redundantly referred to as a CAC card, has storage areas that can be used to store credentials, such as a certificate, and may also be used with additional forms of authentication such as a Personal Identification Number (PIN). Other hardware-based tokens are now in common use as well, one of the better known being the RSA SecureID token. One of the main keys to the future of authentication is the use of biometric identifiers, such as fingerprints, iris scans, and other means based on physical attributes. Such identifiers are ubiquitous, portable, and difficult to forge, given properly designed authentication systems.

Once we have authenticated an identity, we can then check to see what activities that particular identity is allowed to carry out, known as authorization. We can see a common example of authorization in the different levels of account functionality that are defined in many operating systems. Where a root or administrator level account might be authorized to create additional accounts on a system, a general user will likely not be able to do so. In the military it this is normally tied to the commander of a unit who has the ultimate authority.

> **NOTE**
>
> The Principle of Least Privilege states that for any given layer in a computing environment, such as a person, process, or a system, that layer be given only the minimum level of privilege that is needed for it to operate properly. Following this principle negates many of the common security issues that we might face, many of which are due to abuse of inappropriately permissive systems or applications.

Auditing gives us the capability to monitor what activities have taken place on a given system or in an environment. While authentication and authorization allow us to control and set limits on user access to our assets, we also need to keep a record of what these authorized individuals have done. This allows us to balance system and network loads properly, as well as monitor for authorized but inappropriate or unwanted activities. As the attackers continue to develop more capabilities and the networks become more cloud- and mobile-based it will become imperative to allocate resources against detecting where they have gained access.

SECURITY AWARENESS AND TRAINING

People pose what is likely the single largest security vulnerability that we have, or will ever have, in any given system or environment. With most other security problems we can apply a patch, change a configuration, or pile on additional security infrastructure in order to fix the problem. With people, we unfortunately cannot do this. People can be lazy, careless, or simply make honest mistakes, all the while circumventing the carefully planned security measures from the inside and leaving us wide open to attack. This lack of situational awareness of the risk or potential impacts of their actions can be addressed by instilling discipline and understanding through rigorous training. The training should start at the command level so the organizations environment reflects the command climate on cybersecurity.

Although we can attempt to apply technical measures to keep untoward activity from taking place, and we can create policy that clearly points out correct and incorrect behavior, such measures will be for naught if we do not impress upon people some small measure of awareness regarding the issues surrounding security, and train them in the proper behaviors that will keep them and the organization in which they operate on a better security footing. Again these policies must be consistently enforced and understood at all levels of the organization to be effective.

Awareness

Security awareness can be a difficult mode of thinking to those that do not already have some acquaintance with the basic concept. Bruce Schneier wrote a piece on this for Wired magazine in 2008, and called this sort of awareness the security mindset. Schneier said "Security requires a particular mindset. Security professionals—at least the good ones—see the world differently. They can't walk into a store without noticing how they might shoplift. They can't use a computer without wondering about the security vulnerabilities. They can't vote without trying to figure out how to vote twice. They just can't help it" [5].

This security aware mindset is not only critical for security professionals, system administrators, network engineers, and others employed in technical fields, it is also important for combat arms soldiers, aircraft crews, sailors, and their families, etc… handle information that could in any way be considered important or sensitive. To exacerbate the situation, evaluating which data may or may not be sensitive, and in what situations we need to be aware of the security implications of our actions is a function of security awareness, and needs to be taught as well.

To illustrate the consequences of such failures in both judgment and in the proper mindset, we need only to look at the near daily security breaches that appear in the media. One good example of such a failure occurred during the time before the 2008 US presidential election. Workers at the US Department of State were discovered to have repeatedly accessed the passport records in an unauthorized fashion for three people who were, at the time, presidential candidates: Barrack Obama, Hillary Clinton, and John McCain. The systems containing this information are configured to alert a supervisor when the record of a high-profile individual, such as a presidential candidate, is accessed without a legitimate reason.

As a result of this incident, several workers were fired or reprimanded, and those that remained had limitations placed on their access [6]. A modicum of security awareness might have alerted these individuals to the idea that unauthorized access to records containing the personal information of presidential candidates including name, address, date of birth, social security number, travel records, and a variety of other information might have unwanted consequences for them on a personal level.

Our example, while an apt illustration of lack of security awareness, unfortunately falls toward the relatively tame end of the spectrum, as incidents of this type may result in much more impactful situations. Numerous such cases, such as the VA laptop loss that we mentioned when we discussed CIA earlier in this chapter, can be found, from Personally Identifiable Information (PII), such as social security numbers, being broadcast to large email distribution lists to unencrypted medical records of US military veterans being lost, and virtually limitless other cases. While technical security measures can be put in place to help prevent such occurrences, as long as we continue to fail in the aspect of security awareness we will continue to have these issues.

When we attempt to teach these concepts to our users, the main point is simple; try to think like an attacker. In any given situation, whether it is a phishing email, social engineering attack, policy violation, or most any other issue that we may be confronted with, such guidance will usually steer us to the proper path. If we are able to instill a certain amount of constructive suspicion in our user base, we will often find ourselves on the proper side of such incidents. Although we may find that we tend to receive the occasional false positive from training our users in such a fashion, this is a far more desirable result that dealing with the security breaches that come from lack of care in such matters.

Training

In addition to the concepts of security awareness that we wish to instill, there is also the matter of general security training. In most organizations, such training for end users will consist of more specific direction to accompany our general security awareness efforts. In many governmental organizations, such training is mandatory on a reoccurring basis and is tied to Operations Security (OPSEC) and Counter Espionage covered in Chapter 6. Such training will often consist of instruction in properly secure behavior for use of various means of communication such as email, Instant Messenger (IM), phone, etc. These communications media are often used to scam or attempt to elicit information through social engineering, and are an important focus of our security training efforts. Additionally, depending on the environment in question, we may also wish to add additional items to our security training efforts, such as physical security, proper handling of sensitive information, and background checks. One area that is new to this field is the need for training around social media.

When conducting training for the more technical members of an organization, such as system administrators, network engineers, developers, security personnel, and the like, it is still important to go over the basics of our security training program, but we will likely need to compose additional training to address the specifics of such categories of specialization. For our system administrators and network engineers we will need to address the security of our operating systems and network infrastructure, for our developers we will need to address secure coding standards and practices, and for our security personnel we will need to make them aware of both the internal and external security practices of the organization. For all of these members, we need to stress the appropriate use and safeguarding of any privileged accounts to which they may have access. By the end of the training a strong understanding of risk and security mindset should be instilled.

DEFENDING AGAINST CYBER ATTACKS

When defending against cyber attacks, many of the steps that we will take will be proactive in nature and involve hardening our environments and monitoring the activities that take place in them. This is an easy statement to make, and is relatively simple to accomplish in a small or medium sized network environment, relatively speaking, much as what we might find in a business or corporation. When we look to perform such activities in the much larger environment that we might find when operating on a national or a global scale, this becomes a considerably more difficult prospect.

At present, the tools exist perform a certain amount of monitoring on a large scale, as we discussed in the Surveillance section of Chapter 5 but they can be cost prohibitive to smaller organizations. When we begin to look to more specific activities, such as intrusion detection or vulnerability assessment, the scale of environment within which we can cope shrinks to a much smaller set due to the sheer mass of data to be monitored. Presently, strategies are being developed in an attempt to monitor and address large scale cyber attacks, but these are still in their infancy. Currently, much of the effort being put into CND is in the areas of policy and compliance, particularly in governmental circles.

At the time of this writing, the US government was debating whether to give the President the power to sever the entire country or portions of it, from the Internet in the face of a major cyber crisis [7]. In the face of a concerted attack on critical infrastructure, some say that such measures may be preferable to potential destruction and loss of life that could accompany an attack on Supervisory Control and Data Acquisition (SCADA) systems and the environments they control. This may not be an ideal solution, and will likely be exceedingly difficult to carry out. Although not necessarily a viable plan, this and the many other cyber legislations effort serve as a good indicator of the present state of nationwide concern about CND in the US.

Policy and Compliance

One of the major keys to a successful defense lies in the area of security policy. Through the use of policies we can set the expectations for those that develop and use the environments that we expect to keep secured. Security policy defines the behavior of our users, the configuration of our software, systems, and networks, and innumerable other items. Ultimately our security policies define what exactly we mean when we say secure. Additionally, it is important to note that policy implemented without the proper authority to enforce it is utterly useless and often ignored.

In addition to defining our security through policy, we also need to ensure that the policy is followed, this being done through our compliance efforts. In government, compliance is verified against such bodies such as the Federal Information Security Management Act (FISMA), the Department of Defense Information Assurance Certification and Accreditation Process (DIACAP), the National Industrial Security Program Operating Manual (NISPOM), Director of Central Intelligence Directive (DCID) 6/3, and innumerable others. In the civilian world, we find the focus more in the direction of the Health Insurance Portability and Accountability Act (HIPAA), the Payment Card Industry Data Security Standard (PCI DSS), Sarbanes–Oxley (SOX), North American Electric Reliability Corporation (NERC) critical infrastructure protection (CIP) regulations, and many others. Without compliance, our policies are not worth the paper on which they are printed, or the bits in which they are stored. That said it is also important to understand security doesn't stop when compliance is established, it is the baseline not the end state.

Surveillance, Data Mining, and Pattern Matching

As we discussed in the Surveillance section of Chapter 5, many large governments presently have some sort of monitoring on the various means of communications moving in and out of their borders. While this by no means represents complete coverage and gaps in such monitoring can, in many cases, be found or created, it

> **WARNING**
>
> Surveillance and reconnaissance activities, if not conducted properly, can often violate the relevant wiretap laws of the country in which they are carried out. It is important to secure the proper legal advice before proceeding with such efforts.

does provide a measure of security. The ability to track communications with those in other countries can potentially give us a warning when coordinated activities, such as attacks, may be taking place in the immediate future, possibly including cyber attacks, through data mining and pattern matching performed on the communications records we collect.

If we examine the systems that are used to perform large scale communications monitoring, we can see many parallels to the familiar Intrusion Detection Systems (IDS) that we can commonly find in operation on networks. In essence, these systems are IDS operating on a much more gross scale. Such systems may very well serve as the basis or technological precursors for large scale IDS that is capable of the detailed examination of electronic communications that we are familiar with on a small scale. Although the level of technical sophistication needed to perform such activities is lacking at present and could be classified when developed, we are almost certain to see such capabilities in the near future.

Intrusion Detection and Prevention

Intrusion detection and intrusion prevention on a nationwide scale or even across the DoD, as we discussed in the previous section, is a difficult prospect. At present, the networks that comprise the Internet are not segmented along national boundaries, for the most part. Additionally, we have a wide variety of media that can be used to carry network communications, including: copper and fiber optic cables, satellite communications, purpose build wireless networks, packet radio, and any number of other means. This lack of network segmentation along physical borders and wide variety of communications methods makes IDS/IPS a technically challenging prospect to implement.

Two main strategies exist for accomplishing intrusion detection and/or prevention on this scale; we can either structure networks to provide a limited number of connections outside of the area that we wish to protect and monitor, or we implement massively distributed IDS/IPS; either method has its inherent issues. Restructuring our networks to provide only a few choke points is most certainly the cleanest route to take, and may be workable when building new networks, but would likely be prohibitively expensive for existing networks. It will also be impacted by the move to the cloud and mobile devices, the days of isolated networks is even coming to a close in classified networks as we see them looking at how to move to these new infrastructures. Likewise, massively distributed IDS/IPS, although having the benefit of not requiring us to alter our networks, is likely to miss some of the traffic entering and exiting said networks. In either case, at present, conducting such operations is likely to prove difficult in a variety of ways.

Vulnerability Assessment and Penetration Testing

Vulnerability Assessment and Penetration Testing are two of the key tools of CND. These methods allow us to discover the weaknesses in our systems and networks that allow attackers to conduct reconnaissance and surveillance, gain entry, or conduct other attacks.

Vulnerability Assessment allow us to, generally using scanning tools such as those that we discussed in Chapter 5, to discover surface vulnerabilities in our systems. Typically such assessments involve iterating through the complete catalog of our systems and scanning for vulnerabilities on each, using known signatures for those vulnerabilities. While this can indeed expose some of the means of entry that attackers can use, it is not a complete picture of how our systems might be vulnerable. In order to get a more complete picture of the holes in our systems, we need to be much more thorough in our efforts and conduct penetration tests.

Penetration Testing, when conducted properly, can much more closely mirror the activities of an attacker attempting to compromise our environment. Penetration Testing can be performed from a white box perspective, in which we are provided with information on the environment to be attacked, or can be done from a black box perspective, in which we have no additional information than an attacker would normally have. Many arguments can be made for either approach, but generally white box testing is less costly and black box testing more closely represents an outside attack. We may also wish to consider additional elements in our Penetration Testing should include efforts, such as social engineering, which we discussed in Chapter 6, and physical security, which we discussed in Chapter 4.

One of the dangers in planning and in trusting the results of penetration tests is to insure that they are not hampered to the point of not being useful. If we put restrictions on our penetration tests that disallow specific attacks, open source tools, environments, weapon systems, or even legacy systems, then we are no longer accomplishing the goal of using the same methods that potential attackers will be using. This is true in both real-world testing and military exercises. Such restrictions are all too common in penetration testing scenarios and can not only render our efforts useless, but can provide us with a false sense of security.

Disaster Recovery Planning

Disaster Recovery Planning (DRP), as a defensive measure, can allow us to withstand or recover from the attacks, outages, and disasters that we were not able to prevent outright. Such measures are usually accomplished through the use of backups for our data and through the use of varying degrees of redundant systems and infrastructure. Although, in the case of CND, properly stored backups will certainly allow us to recover in the case of an attack, it is more likely that we will find greater utility in redundant infrastructure to resist an attack.

In the case of a large scale cyber attack, it is entirely possible that we will find ourselves unable to operate from certain network blocks, domains, systems, etc…Unlike the disaster recover planning that most organizations undertake, when undertaking such planning for CND, it will more than likely pay to ensure that our backup locations from which we can operate are distributed widely in both a geographical and a logical sense. In this way, when we are under attack or need to operate from a logically separated location, we are likely to have one which has not been affected by the attack. This can be challenging with forward deployed units so contingency plans like Continuity of Operations (COOP) must be developed so the units can continue the mission under degraded or denied network conditions.

Defense in Depth

One of the more important principles of a successful defensive strategy is defense in depth. Defense in depth proposes a layered approach to security, as shown in Figure 7.3. In this particular case we have defenses at the network level, the host level, the application level, and the data level. We might have, as an example, firewalls and IDS/IPS at the network level, software firewalls and anti-malware tools at the host level, access controls at the application level, and encryption at the data level. In addition, the user awareness training we talked about in the security aware-ness section of this chapter could easily be integrated into our layers of security. At the center of all these layers of defense lies our critical information. The layers and security measures at each layer may vary according to the environment in question, but the basic principles will remain the same.

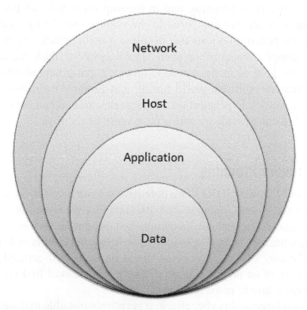

FIGURE 7.3 Defense in Depth

> **NOTE**
>
> Defense in depth is actually an ancient military concept. One of the first recorded uses of such a strategy was carried out by Hannibal against the Romans during the Battle of Cannae in 216 B.C. [8].

The principle behind defense in depth is, through the multiple layers of security measures, to hinder our attackers sufficiently so that our elements of detection will discover their activities or so that they will decide that our security measures are too great and give up on their attacks. As we move to a more mobile device-based network this principle is still critical it is just that the layers of defense are on the endpoint system not the central network.

We may like to think that we can create an environment that is impenetrable to attack and can successfully fend off any attacker for an indefinite period of time, but this is an unrealistic expectation. Instead, we should configure our layered defenses so that we can slow an attacker as much as we can in order to have time to detect and deal with their attacks. Additionally, if we segment the information on the network properly, and restrict access to each segment based on need, we can help mitigate more of the risk of an attacker being able to get in, get everything, and get back out again.

SUMMARY

In this chapter, we discussed Computer Network Defense (CND). CND is the defensive and largely proactive component of Computer Network Operations (CNO). We discussed how CND fits into the overall category of defensive actions and how non-nation states might not have sufficient resources to be able to defend against a complete attack by a nation state.

We covered what exactly it is that we attempt to secure, in the sense of data and information. We also covered some of the key principles of security such as the CIA triad of confidentiality, integrity, and availability, as well as AAA, covering authentication, authorization, and auditing. These basic principles are the foundations on which we base the defense of our information assets.

We talked about security awareness and training efforts in order to secure what is likely to be the weakest link in our defenses; people. We covered the security mindset, and what we can try to do to impart some of this mindset to the users for which we are responsible. Then we covered security training for our users, so that we might educate them as to the proper responses for some of the situations in which they might potentially damage our security footing. We also discussed the need for differing security training for the different levels of technical ability that we might need to address.

In defending against cyber attacks, we talked about some of the different strategies that we might use to defend ourselves against attack. We covered some of the uses that the surveillance tactics from Computer Network Exploit (CNE) might be put to use and how data mining and pattern matching might be used on such collected data. We also covered intrusion detection and intrusion prevention and how implementing these on a very large scale might be difficult. We discussed the uses of vulnerability assessment and penetration testing in discovering the security holes in our environments, and some of the ways in which such tactics might provide us a false sense of security. We went over disaster recovery planning and how we might need to customize such plans to cope with the realities of cyber warfare. Lastly, we looked at defense in depth and discussed how we might employ many layered security measures in our defensive implementations.

In Computer Network Defense we have to be successful, all the time and every time. Our opponents can attack at any time, using any method at their disposal, and only need to be successful once. We have to be alert and react to every attack. This applies to every system, network, and organization equally. As a part of the military, critical infrastructure, or even corporate systems, you are part of the ongoing fight…

REFERENCES

[1] Cyberspace & Information Operations Study Center. What are information operations? Cyberspace and information operations study center; July 24, 2010 [online, cited May 28, 2012]. <http://www.au.af.mil/info-ops/what.htm>.

[2] Arrington Michael. Google defends against large scale Chinese cyber attack: may cease Chinese operations. TechCrunch; January 12, 2010 [online, cited May 28, 2012]. <http://techcrunch.com/2010/01/12/google-china-attacks/>.

[3] Nagesh Gautham. VA loses another laptop with veterans' personal data, prompting inquiry. The Hill; May 13, 2010 [online, cited May 28, 2012]. <http://thehill.com/blogs/hillicon-valley/technology/97817-va-loses-another-laptop-with-veterans-personal-information>.

[4] Parker Donn. Fighting computer crime. s.l., Wiley; 1998. ISBN 0471163783.

[5] Schneier Bruce. Inside the twisted mind of the security professional. Wired.com; March 20, 2008 [online, cited May 28, 2012]. <http://www.wired.com/politics/security/commentary/securitymatters/2008/03/securitymatters_0320>.

[6] Associated Press. Passport files of candidates breached. MSNBC.com; March 21, 2008 [online, cited May 28, 2012]. <http://www.msnbc.msn.com/id/23736254/>.

[7] Schwartz Matthew. Schwartz on security: Zombie Internet 'Kill Switch'. Information week; October 28, 2010 [online, cited May 28, 2012]. <http://www.informationweek.com/news/security/management/showArticle.jhtml?articleID=228000213>.

[8] Flaherty Kyle. Verifying your defense in depth strategy: from Hannibal to today. BreakingPoint; September 3, 2009 [online, cited May 28, 2012]. <http://www.breakingpointsystems.com/community/blog/verifying-your-defense-in-depth-strategy-from-hannibal-to-today/>.

Challenges We Face

8

INFORMATION IN THIS CHAPTER:

- Cybersecurity Issues Defined
- Interrelationship of Cybersecurity Issues
- Way Ahead

This chapter is based on research conducted for a white paper developed by TASC under the CTO's office CyberAssure™ program. The study was designed to help customers understand the entire set of cyber challenges facing them today so they could determine where resources would best be used. It was done in conjunction with University of Virginia Applied Research Institute. The original authors were Steve Winterfeld, Anthony Gadient, Kent Schlussel, and Alfred Weaver. It is used here with their permission.

Currently, the United States (US), Western Europe, and much of Asia have integrated the Internet into both their economy and military to the point they are dependent on it for daily operations. For the US, these digital capabilities have become a strategic center of gravity. Additionally, most other nations are quickly moving in this direction. The number of systems (computers, mobile devices, infrastructure devices) and applications (stand alone, networked, and web based) that support this cyber capability is growing exponentially. Due to this explosive growth, nations struggle with systems that are plagued with vulnerabilities that could easily impact our ability to maintain confidentiality, validate integrity, and ensure availability. This increasing reliance on technology has created significant national cybersecurity challenges.

At the same time, advanced technologies and tools for computer network operations have become widely available at low cost, resulting in a basic, but operationally significant, technical capability for US adversaries of all types, including hackers (anyone conducting unauthorized activities on a system), insider threat, hacktivists (cause-based hackers), industrial spies, organized crime, terrorists, and national governments (often called Advanced Persistent Threat or APT). President Barack Obama said "It's now clear that this cyber threat is one of the most serious economic

113

and national security challenges we face as a nation. It's also clear that we're not as prepared as we should be, as a government or as a country" [1].

As the TASC team looked at this issue they conducted analysis of numerous studies which identified foundational issues, the authors have added to their original list. There is no single document that succinctly and comprehensively identifies the cyber challenges facing the US and Department of Defense (DoD), and organizes these issues so that both senior leaders can develop a comprehensive plan to address the challenges facing their organizations and technical staff can identify which challenges most impact their organization. This chapter addresses this gap in three ways. First, it provides a concise review and taxonomy of the principal cyber challenges facing the US and DoD. Next it lays out who should allocate resources to the different challenges. Finally it provides a look at the way ahead. It is not designed to provide the answers but rather to start a discussion about the next steps to prepare the US for success in cyberspace.

CYBERSECURITY ISSUES DEFINED

These challenges were analyzed based on a national view point and would need to be changed for specific units or organizations. The issues were selected based on customer feedback, TASC Cyber Community of Excellence input and review of studies like: Institute for Information Infrastructure Protections' (I3P) National Cyber security R&D Challenges [2], Networking and Information Technology Research and Development's (NITRD) National Cyber Leap Year [3], InfoSec's Hard Problem List [4], Computing Research Association's Four Grand Challenges in Trustworthy Computing [5], Department of Energy's A scientific R&D approach to Cybersecurity [6], Center for Strategic and International Studies' (CSIS) Securing Cyberspace for 44th president report [7], Bush's National Cybersecurity Strategy [8], HSPD 54's Comprehensive National Cybersecurity Initiative (CNCI) focus areas [9], Obama's Cyberspace Policy Review [10]. The authors picked the final list based on the major pain points they think our nation is facing. They acknowledge there are subjects that could be argued to be added, while some of the ones included are not critical to some organizations or could be grouped differently.

The authors have categorized each challenge by level of complexity. The rankings are: Extremely Difficult (ED), Very Difficult (VD), Difficult (D), and Not Cost Effective (NCE). There is no clean way to rank them, as the types of resources are different for each challenge, so we have tried to quantify/qualify the complexity and types of resources needed. In some cases it is classic research and development for new technology, for others it is political will, some need regulation and finally, they all need some level of funding.

We have also categorized the challenges by resources required with the following designation by each challenge: Very Significant = $$$, Significant = $$, Less Significant = $. While it is difficult to address how to categorize levels of resources, as different challenges required different methods to solve in general, we will use the initial unclassified CNCI budget of 9 billion as very significant, less than 4 billion as significant and less than 1 billion as less significant. These are very general estimates and each problem would need to be examined against a specific plan to determine resources required.

The challenges are grouped to show their relationships. The major areas are Policy, Technical, and People. The areas of overlap between them are policy and technical has process in common, technical and people has skills in common and people and policy has organizations in common. Then there is a core set that is common to all the challenges (the mapping is shown in Figure 8.1). They are not listed by order of importance as each organization would rank these issues differently based on their risks.

Policy

Laws (ED $) encompass policy, legal issues, national security, and privacy. In the US today, these issues tend to conflict with each other. Our culture and heritage influence

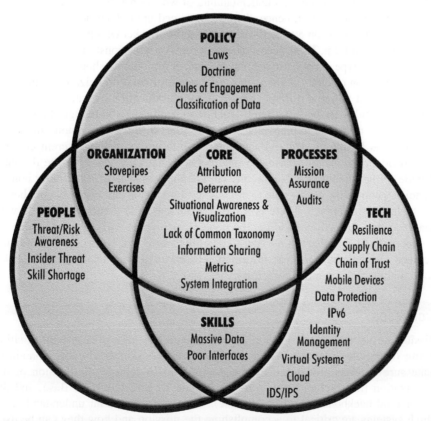

FIGURE 8.1 This Figure Shows the Categorization and Relationships of the Challenges

the formation of our laws. Relatively speaking, cyber issues are new when compared to the backdrop of our legal system (dating from common English law and the Magna Carta in the year 1215). Our legal system lacks experience in setting boundaries for many of the technological advances today, to include cyber, medicine, and advances in communications. The legal issues are further complicated within the US as each state sets its own laws that vary widely and even federal law is interpreted differently in various courts.

Doctrine (VD $) suffers from a lack of consistency across the military services that address offense and defensive cyber strategy through tactics techniques and procedures. This is not to say that there is a complete lack of doctrine or that it conflicts but rather there is no common unifying doctrine. The DoD has made progress by establishing a common set of terms [11]. Also each service has stood up commands and at the Joint level CYBERCOM has been stood up. The problem remains that there is no common vision of cyber operations and cyberspace warfighting doctrine.

Rules of Engagement (ROE) (VD $) is needed for local commanders who understand how to react to real world or kinetic attacks based on approved ROEs, but in cyberspace there is no common understanding of what constitutes a '*use of force*' or '*act of war*' on the Internet, hence, there is no agreed upon doctrine on how to fight a cyber war. If there is an attack, the response to the attacker (if attribution is accomplished) is not uniform. There needs to be clear rules on what constitutes an incident or attack and what type of response (technical, legal, or diplomatic) should be conducted.

Classification of data (D $$) issues are a result of each organization within the US government utilizing different practices for classification of data, creating disconnects in ability to work with non-DoD organizations. Even though there is one official set of rules, the implementation of the rules differ wildly among the many agencies that handle classified documents. Couple that with the different cultures in each organization, the sharing of data between agencies can often be difficult. Outside of the Intelligence Community (IC), the rest of the DoD and other non-IC agencies, people may not be able to discuss certain matters and properly collaborate due to lack of clearance. There is a move to increase the number of people with clearances but that will not address the issue as each crisis will require a unique set of experts to fix and there is no way to determine who will be needed beforehand. We need a system that can share information based on need, not background checks, while maintaining operational security.

Processes

Mission Assurance (ED $$) is the focus on protecting networks and information during operations. There is a need to fight through a contested cyber domain to make sure the operational tasks are accomplished to achieve the mission of the organization (this includes military systems, the Defend Industrial Base, and the commercial backbone networks they use). What is needed is an understanding of which systems are critical to accomplishing the mission and how they can be used in a degraded mode (i.e. using a limited or alternate set of protocols) to continue to maintain maneuverability and basic capabilities in a environment that they may no longer control.

Audits (D $) are the regular, structured evaluation of an enterprise's cyber systems, personnel, and processes. The audit process represents the measurement step in a continuous cybersecurity improvement program (implement → measure → correct). As such, regular cyber audits represent the keystone of any cybersecurity program. However, in a recent cyber audit of the Department of Homeland Security (DHS) performed by the Inspector General (IG); the DHS IG noted that, "Adequate security controls have not been implemented to protect the data processed from unauthorized access, use, disclosure, disruption, modification, or destruction" [12].

Given the recognized importance of the cyber audit as part of any cybersecurity program, we might ask why a cyber audit of the organization chartered with the security of the US homeland would identify over 600 vulnerabilities, including 202 classified as high-risk [13]. The reason is simple. Today there exists no easy way to verify accounts, records, employee activity, and security configurations against a set of well-defined policies. To avoid the type of results obtained by the DHS IG, we need to develop a set of standards that both the government and industry can use as a basis for building an automated cyber auditing capability.

On a slightly different track we have the current set of Certification and Accreditation standards that are used today. The DOD Information Assurance Certification and Accreditation Process (DIACAP) and Director of Central Intelligence Directive (DCID) 6/3 processes as well as the Federal Information System Management Act (FISMA) process for all government agencies is undergoing a change to be more focused on real-time monitoring. The NIST Special Publication 800-137 Information Security Continuous Monitoring for Federal Information Systems and Organizations (Draft Dec 2010) [14] is a great example of where they are headed [15].

Technical

Resilience (ED $$$) is designed to have systems self-heal with no intervention from humans. In the cyber context, a resilient cyber system must continue to operate (as intended) even if compromised—for example, if unauthorized access is achieved. It should be noted that this is different than Continuation of Operations Planning (COOP), Disaster Recovery Planning (DRP), or reconstitution. Given the highly

> **NOTE**
>
> There are a number of standards like Information Systems Audit and Control Association's (ISACA) Control Objectives for Information and related Technology (COBIT), the International Organization for Standardization's Code of Practice for Information Security Management family of standards. These can be supported with processes like Information Technology Infrastructure Library (ITIL), Capability Maturity Model Integration (CMMI), and Six Sigma but there is no common practice today.

distributed nature of cyber systems today, an important aspect of resilience is the ability of a system to meet its specified function in the face of denial of service attacks which might compromise network access. Resilience is therefore an attribute we need our cyber systems to posses, as such—the challenge is to develop a resilient system, and in particular to design an enterprise-level system to be resilient in a contested cyber conflict environment.

Supply Chain (ED $$$) relates to the development and manufacturing of both hardware and software which has increasingly been accomplished in foreign countries. There is very little hardware or software that does not contain foreign components. With the increasing complexity of hardware, the verification and validation of hardware has become very difficult. If we can authenticate all the interactions among the hardware components in a system, then we can verify that the hardware does what it claims to do.

How authentication of hardware and software is done is the challenge. Many hardware components come from many different (and sometime competing) manufacturers and the software or firmware loads are often integrated at different stages of manufacture. Every interface and transaction must be authenticated to insure the device works as advertised and that there are no hidden capabilities that can cause harm to the overall system or create covert channels and unknown vulnerabilities that can be exploited by advisories (be they nation state or criminal).

An example of the challenges that arise from a supply chain is the intentional inclusion of a logic bomb in a hardware implementation by a potential adversary. This is of particular concern given the significant number of integrated circuits that are fabricated in Taiwan and China.

Chain of trust (VD $$) comes from the need for increasing trustworthy computing in an enterprise setting which can occur if we can authenticate all interactions among enterprise hardware supporting the enterprise users' computing needs. Such an approach using hardware that can authenticate every connection prevents or makes much more difficult a man-in-the-middle type of attack. An example would be when a command and control system sends an order to a weapon's system: how does the sender know it was received, how does the receiver know it was really from the command and control system, and how do both know the contents of the message were not modified.

Mobile devices (VD $$) are a challenge as more and more devices connect to the grid (smartphones, thumb drives, iPads, and laptops) there is a need to both protect them and validate their security before the connect. In many cases these devices are being used to conduct sensitive business and connected to protected networks with little to no security monitoring. The younger generation of workers are bringing their technology from home to the work place and doing work on their personal devices and it is becoming a challenge for the security team to keep up to date with what is going on.

IPv6 (D $$) presents a challenge because during the transition to the new protocol there will be new opportunities for both defenders and attackers. In 2012 the Internet

Corporation for Assigned Names and Numbers (ICANN) is predicted to be out of IPv4 Internet Protocol (IP) addresses. This will force implementation of IPv6 over the next couple of years. Most of the challenge will come from upgrading equipment and finding staff with IPv6 skills. With the new protocol comes changes like so many addresses that scanning all the network addresses for an organization will become resource prohibitive which will cause a shift in tactics and tools. So while it is less mature there is more security built into the protocol which means once it is widely implemented it should provide better security.

Data Protection (D $) is the focus on providing confidentiality, integrity, and availability of the data rather than protecting the network or operating system. Today, in a fortress mentality, many organizations focus their cybersecurity efforts on protecting the cyber perimeter using products such as firewalls. This "line in the sand" or "Maginot Line" approach fails to recognize that a significant portion of the value of an organization's cyber assets lies in the data that is stored on their cyber systems. This data includes more than just documents; it also includes emails, web pages, web apps, and key executables such as operating systems. One obstacle many organizations would need to face first is categorizing their data by level or importance/value. Therefore, a comprehensive cyber strategy should place significant emphasis on data protection in addition to any efforts that are applied to perimeter defense. When viewed in this information-centric manner, critical questions arise. We must ask if a perimeter defense is the most appropriate approach to data protection, or is an asymmetric, decentralized, defense required [16]. The answer is no, and the solution is that we need to move to a new model.

Identity Management (IDM) (NCE $$) consists of three functions that need to be accomplished when allowing personnel to access the network: authenticate—they are who they say they are, authorize—what they have access to, and audit—what they do. The days of IDM being just a 8–12 character password are dead. Today most companies are moving to tokens or biometrics to help ensure they are authenticating the individual. They are also building rules that limit what each individual can do so they only have access to what they need to do their jobs. The issue is that there is no common standard today. There are effort like the DHS who has published a draft of the National Strategy for Trusted Identities in Cyberspace [17] which could help at the national level.

Virtual Systems (NCE $)/Cloud (NCE $) may occur at many levels (e.g. hardware, memory, storage, software, data, desktop, network, or entire data centers). Virtualization at the level of the operating system (OS) permits the hosting of multiple virtualized environments within a single OS instance. Applications can be virtualized, allowing them to be hosted independently of the underlying OS. Cross-platform virtualization allows software written for a specific central processing unit (CPU) and OS to nevertheless operate on different CPUs and OSs. At the top level of abstraction, a Virtual Machine (VM) is a software implementation of an operating system or computer. At the network level, virtualization allows access to applications, data, and computing resources through the Internet (also known as "cloud computing").

TIP

When dealing with a vendor selling cloud services it is important to understand there are three primary cloud-based delivery models. Be sure you're getting the right one for your organization.

- *Software as a Service (SaaS):* The user accesses applications that are on the network.
- *Platform as a Service (PaaS):* The user uses the cloud as an environment for executing applications. This is the opposite approach from SaaS, because users control their applications but have no control over the environment on which their applications execute.
- *Infrastructure as a Service (IaaS):* This is an even higher level of abstraction. Rather than purchasing physical resources, the user accesses the necessary resources as a service from a third party, typically on a pay-per-use basis.

For reasons of security and governance, clouds can be deployed as public, private, or hybrid. Public clouds are those data centers outside a user's firewall and are provided by third-parties. Private clouds remain within a user's firewall; hybrid clouds offer a mixture of both.

From a security point of view, virtualization has issues with configuration management, patching, cross-platform attacks, and auditing. Cloud computing has issues with shifting applications, data management, and processes to a third party set of configuration standards, control/ownership over sensitive data, reliability of company hosting the data, applicable laws, and lack of physical control. Security and confidentiality are crucial issues for successful transition to these technologies. In addition, there are legitimate concerns over performance variability, reliability, and resilience of cloud-based services.

Intrusion Detection Systems (IDS)/Intrusion Protection Systems (IPS) (NCE $$) monitor the network to detect signatures of known malware or patterns of activity that are unauthorized. Today, significant attention is paid to protecting our IT systems to prevent intrusion. The philosophy underlying this is that if only authorized individuals have access to the cyber systems, those systems are to a large degree protected. The philosophy driving interest in intrusion detection is that if no intrusion is detected, then it can be inferred that only authorized individuals are accessing the system and the system is de-facto safe (clearly, per our earlier discussions, insider threat does not go away). However, ignoring the challenges represented by Insider Threat, Intrusion Detection is in itself a challenging problem. Today most security detection systems are signature based, yet signature-based defenses are inherently perimeter focused and state-of-the-art cyber threats tunnel through or go around these defenses. Also, Intrusion Detection systems only show what they catch, not what they are not catching, so if there is no signature in place, the attack may go completely unnoticed. Looking forward we must detect and protect against zero-day exploits.

Skills

Massive Data (VD $$) is the result of so much data being collected that there needs to be a way to stop data mining and start real-time correlation. Today logging is a challenge; the classic debate is how much needs to be done because it raises costs. Most large networks (over 10,000 users) don't have the resources to log more than a few weeks worth of data and even that is not truly analyzed. We need systems and processes that allow us to do long term trend analysis (over months not just days or weeks).

Poor Interfaces (D $) are problematic as most systems are not designed to allow a user to rapidly manipulate information at the rate it is coming into the database. Those who have ever been in a Security Operations Center know it is not unusual to see Intrusion Detection System (IDS) events scrolling off the screen. We need security systems that are intuitive and allow the analysis to develop and manage the investigations in a way that they provide an advantage rather than just a person to react to what they are provided.

People

Threat/Risk Awareness (ED $$) is a concern because most users today implicitly trust their computer system when they log on, they assume emails are actually sent from the displayed sender and they don't think attachments like word documents could contain malware. This behavior issue must be addressed. We need to change the mindset of the user to "trust but verify" when they log on. Users should understand how to validate their security and know what kind of indicators to look for in a compromised system. We don't expect everyone to become a cybersecurity expert but we do want them to have basic survival skills to keep their information secure. One simple example is to use encrypted email when discussing sensitive material. There needs to be a national program, for awareness it could be based on the "Smokey the bear says—stop forest fires" or "This is your brain on drugs" campaigns.

Insider Threat (NCE $$) is quite possibly the greatest challenge. The definition of who is an insider has been debated. Most people automatically think an insider is an employee, a student, or other member of the staff of a host institution that physically operates a computer system. These people have a legitimate reason to access the cyber systems and can be considered insiders. However, it can be many other types of people:

- A contractor, associate, business partner, etc…, someone who has a business relationship with the institution that hosts the computer system.
- An authorized person that is allowed to perform limited operations (e.g. a bank's customer who uses the bank's system to access his/her account or a student who is allowed to access grades).
- A person who has been coerced or duped into performing certain operations on an outsider's behalf.
- A former insider possessing access credentials that were not revoked when terminated.
- A former insider who created "secret" credentials to give his/her access at a later date.

There are many reasons why a person behaves in a malicious manner. Some of these are for ideological reasons: revenge, ego that proves the insider can just do it, and plain greed. While people have not significantly changed in the last 20 years, the technical and economic landscape of the US has changed significantly. Technology advances and e-commerce has made it easier for the insider to gain access to critical information [18]. This problem will continue to get more complex as the world becomes more interconnected. We need to increase our ability to use role-based management and real-time auditing.

Skill Shortage (NCE $$$) is influenced by the general lack of skilled cybersecurity engineers today and the poor pipeline for new talent coming out of the schools. In the report Human Capital Crisis in Cybersecurity Jim Glosler a NSA visiting scientist and founding director of the CIA's Clandestine Information Technology Office was quoted saying "There are only about 1000 security specialists in the US who have the specialized skills to operate effectively in cyberspace: however the US needs about 10,000–30,000 such individuals." There is a severe shortage of skilled cybersecurity professionals to address the needs of the force today, as many of the US's top cybersecurity minds are "unclearable" or have no interest in working for the government or the military. Also, educational programs focusing on cybersecurity at institutions of higher learning are still in their infancy. In March of 2010 the administration did kick off the National Initiative for Cybersecurity Education (NICE) [20] and DHS/NSA has the Centers of Academic Excellence in Information Assurance Education [21] but there is no national-level effort.

Organization

Stovepipes (D $) are built around Computer Network Operations (CNO) functions and while it may be easy to separate different "disciplines" of cybersecurity for discussion points, they are all inter-related to one another in practice. When we look at Computer Network Operations, which consist of Computer Network Attack (CNA), Computer Network Defense (CND), and Computer Network Exploitation (CNE), we see them treated as separate disciplines and there is little to no crosstalk or collaboration. All three disciplines need to integrate the offense (CNA) with the defense (CND) and enable them with intelligence (CNE). The DoD does this today in the kinetic world and needs to apply the same processes to the virtual battle space across the different organizations that control these capabilities. There are

---

WARNING

The WikiLeaks case involving US diplomatic cables [19] was the act of an insider that posed a new kind of threat. In the past we had people who were disgruntled, or had criminal intent, but now whistleblowers and hacktivists pose a new danger. This breach of confidentiality could impact political systems, financial systems, and average companies with sensitive material. It requires a new set of processes, skills, and tools to address.

also stovepipes built along budget or organizational structures but this issue is aimed at integration of CNO.

Exercises (D $$) challenges are based on need to practice responses to every situation. This is increasingly the case when applied to organizations. When we look at the number and types of exercises today there is simply a lack of both focused and integrated exercises to understand the responses to a cyber event. Generally, the rules that limit current cyber exercises do not accurately reflect the level of impact cyber is expected to play in a real-world conflict so organizations are not training as they expect to fight. So if cyber is considered to be another domain of warfare (others being land, sea, air, space), there has been no unifying doctrine to understand the various aspects of "cyberspace" or Tactics Techniques and Procedures (TTPs) that would come out of exercises. Note that there are some efforts like Cyber ShockWave and Cyber Storm but cyber needs to become a ubiquitous aspect of exercises.

Core (Impacting All Areas)

Attribution (ED $$$) for cyber is the process of determining who conducted an activity. There are three types of attribution in cyberspace: geolocation (facilitates kinetic military type strike), tracking a cyber identity (facilitates the intelligence community tracking activity of a specific person or group), or tie a person to the keyboard (facilitates a criminal investigation). It is worth noting there are many technical attribution capabilities that are not allowed due to policy or legal restrictions.

The ability to identify, beyond a reasonable doubt, the originator of a cyber attack is essential to enable an effective and legal response. Given the virtual nature of the cyber challenge, collection of forensic evidence takes on a new life—what is the cyber equivalent of a fingerprint or DNA? What does the "reasonable doubt" threshold mean in a virtual world? To complicate things further, if investigators are able to trace an attack, what can be done with the results? For the military what level of intelligence is sufficient to authorize and attack? Fundamentally, today there exists no way to reliably identify the original attacker.

In his testimony before Congress, General Alexander stated that: "Conflict in cyberspace, moreover, is highly asymmetric. Minor actors can afford and deploy tools to magnify their effects; witness the recent press reports about arrests in Europe of several individuals charged with creating the so-called "Mariposa botnet"—a collection of 13 million computers slaved together for criminal purposes. The tools these actors can employ are almost anonymous—a defender can sometimes learn where an attack came from, but can be time-consuming. That means "attribution" in cyberspace is costly and comparatively rare. The "price" an adversary pays for a capability—a tool or weapon—can be slight; the cost and impact borne by the victim of the attack can be very high" [22].

Deterrence (ED $) is associated with what will happen if we launch a cyber attack or practices poor cyber behavior. Deterrence only occurs when there is something—a legal rule, cultural taboo, or consequence—that makes us not "attack" a system, knowing full well what happens when we get "caught." The most critical aspect of

Deterrence is to make the cost/benefit ratio change from today's high benefits and low cost or risk to us where the costs outweigh the benefits. This can be accomplished by making the cost of the attack very high by either increasing the barriers so that an effective attack requires significantly more resources to perpetrate, or by increasing the cost of retaliation by improving the chance of detection.

Situational Awareness & Visualization (ED $$) is the correlation and fusion of data from multiple sources that enables decision making. This is, at best, poorly understood today. Situational awareness allows leaders to make informed decisions. There are many Common Operational Pictures (COP) and dashboards today, but they fail to facilitate true risk posture understanding and/or provide information in a format that enables decisions. If the data does not facilitate a decision it will soon be ignored. The types of data and their presentation should be driven by the types of decisions that must be made. It will vary at different levels of an organization and for different functions within any organizational level but today they are driven by the type of data available. First the roles need to be set, we must understand what decisions need to be supported and finally the standards for implementing how we present information to the different audiences needs to be established.

Lack of common Taxonomy (VD $) issues revolve around the need for a standard "language" for cyber topics. When we read or discuss computer security, network security, InfoSec, Information Assurance, cybersecurity, or cyber war, we must be careful to understand the terms that are being used and that everyone is using the same definition. There is no industry standard, government regulation, or international agreement on what is meant by simple terminology like "intrusion". This can quickly lead to confusion when trying to have a diverse group of professionals analyze an incident. Within DoD there was so much confusion on what malware was called they hired MITRE to establish a Common Vulnerabilities and Exposures (CVE) [23] database. There needs to be an international body that determines the definitions for IT terms that will be used by the technical community, governments, and the legal authorities.

Information Sharing (D $$) is a challenge in the sense that people like to share most information with the exception of what they believe to be private. However this is not the case for governments and corporations. Corporations often do not share information simply due to competition, and governments do not share information for matters of national security. In the cyber world, the question arises whether corporations and governments should share information on cyber attacks.

However, there are cases where we may want to keep cybersecurity issues limited to a few key personnel. Some examples of these cases are: don't want to expose a vulnerability, desire to protect reputation, need to limit liability or cost of participation in external investigation. Efforts in one area often do not share information with efforts in another despite being inter-related. Knowledge transfer in a large organization is more difficult due to the size and communications flow. There are also a number of public/private efforts that the government is trying to get industry to share information but these efforts are not coordinated and many of them are only achieving limited success.

Metrics (D $) revolve around the need to quantify the impact of malicious and suspicious cyber activity. Just as there is no common understanding of definitions for cyber topics, there also exists no set of predefined, industry standard metrics for cyber activities. Metrics for cyber are difficult to implement because of varying definitions of what is needed and important. For example, how we measure Return on Investment (ROI) is varied based on what organizations see as important. There are three basic types of metrics:

- *Technical:* Most organizations track how many intrusion attempts were stopped, how many viruses were detected, number of days/hours systems were up, communications exchanged (email, IM), number of incidents closed out.
- *Security:* If an organization introduced new processes to detect intrusions that increased detection by 20% or lowered cost by $50,000, or introduced a new tool in the Security Operations Center that cut time to accredit systems by 17 weeks. These goals must be set before the change and methods to track performance are established.
- *Risk Posture:* Examples include: when an organization is connected to new partner networks and it impacted our risk by 40% or our external router was compromised and it lowered our security posture to yellow because it forced us to change the access control list to block IP ranges that were attacking us without normal configuration control processes.

There are many groups working on this issue to include the Administration's CIO's IT Dashboard and the IT Workforce Committee's Importance of Effective Performance Metrics studies, but these are not getting the level of wide acceptance needed [24]. The solution may be regulatory, legislative or industry best practices, but there needs to be a standard so we can measure the impact and benefits of our actions.

System Integration (D $$) is the desire to overcome the common practice today of an organizations purchasing multiple point security systems that do not work together and instead, get one system that coordinates and correlates protection activities. Most security systems used today have a specific function. For example, an organization may have a firewall, an intrusion detection system, anti-virus and anti-spyware tools, forensics tools to help with attribution, network management and monitoring systems including packet sniffers, encryption/decryption capabilities, virtual private networks, patch management systems, web activity filtering, password, and log activity correlation. Each of these systems produces logs which need to be correlated together to provide a view of the overall system health and risk posture. This type of correlation is only possible through the appropriate integration of our subsystems and essential to address a variety of cyber threats including the ability to identify and track potential insider threats. However, too often today's subsystems act as a series of point tools that do not interact to achieve the synergistic effects integration can provide.

It should be noted that, while systems integration can provide numerous benefits, including enabling a more complete and integrated operational picture of the cyber threat, it also increases the risk that, like dominos, an effective cyber attack that brings down one subsystem causes the entire system to fail. This highlights the importance and need for resilience and represents an important challenge in architecting the cyber enterprise. Just as in insurgency warfare, there is a trade-off between pushing down control to the lowest levels to allow small units to act independently versus having more centralized control to enable larger coordinated efforts. Likewise, the architecting of a robust cyber enterprise faces similar challenges. We cannot continue to have multiple point solutions, we need a unified framework.

INTERRELATIONSHIP OF CYBERSECURITY ISSUES

Many of these issues are interdependent. We will follow some examples of how they are tied together. The following examples will highlight some of the inter-relationships between the issues.

Deterrence is something the US uses as a foundational part of their foreign relations policy. There have been many discussions about how this principle can be applied to cyberspace. Before we can begin to utilize it we require attribution pointing to a specific individual, group, or nation that is responsible. If we are able to solve this (through use of all our intelligence capabilities) we would still need clear policies on our reaction, military doctrine and ROE showing our responses. This would not be a simple if A then B equation like the Nuclear Mutually Assured Destruction (MAD) policy as there is a wide range of factors that could come into play. It would be more like a complex matrix of options which is hard to use as deterrence because the response is often not clear.

Military ROE is complex for the same reasons deterrence is difficult. There would need to be a clear set of actions with easily understandable reactions preauthorized. National policy, supporting laws and doctrine would all need to be established. Finally standards of attribution would need to be determined so commanders could know when they had enough intelligence (military normally acts on intelligence and does not determine if there is enough evidence) to act.

Mobile devices would require a set of common interfaces to allow system integration. There are so many proprietary systems using unique protocols and configuration that it is not practical or cost efficient to have one network operations center or security operations center try and manage them all. Some advancement in systems integration is needed to allow the management of all the devices being introduced to networks every year.

Audits are becoming critical to risk management, but it depends on developing industry standards. Before these standards can be created we need to baseline the identity management systems, agree on what metrics will be analyzed and document the definitions of everything involved.

Stovepipes are tied to Classification of Data. Stovepipes are organization-based issues but culture of classification of data is normally set inside the same stovepipe. Once a culture of sharing is established and the walls are broken down the culture of what can reasonably be declassified will allow the release of a lot of information. It is important to note that insider threat is also a key concern when establishing a functional system for sharing information—auditing and good identity management (both authentication and authorization) are the foundation for building a system that allows safe sharing of information.

Situational Awareness is the "holy grail" for many large networks. It can mean understanding what the attacker's intent is, what they have done after they got in, how an event has changed the risk posture of the network, what the impact to mission capabilities, or identifying who it was that penetrated the network. Each of these questions requires a slightly different set of data to answer the question. For some it is just correlation of the integrated systems, for others it is metrics, some require internal auditing, a number of them want attribution. The data must facilitate a decision and be presented visually in an intuitive manner.

Insider threat needs policy support, auditing, and identity management. First privacy issues need to be addressed. Then we have to find a cost effective way to track activity of all users and be able to recognize malicious behavior. Finally we have to be able to positively identify who took which actions. These must all be solved in a standardized and cost effective way which requires solving the auditing set of issues and situational awareness issues.

Then there are the issues that involve multiple challenges. To some degree they are all impacted by lack of taxonomy, metrics, and the standard rules (doctrine, policy, regulations, procedures, laws…). It is very difficult to have a discussion about the solution if there is not a common baseline on the meanings of terms and methods or measurement much less without common set of guidelines everyone will follow. Finally supply chain underlies all of the technical issues. If we cannot have confidence in our hardware or software then nothing that happens can be believed.

WAY AHEAD

With limited resources what should we focus on? Some of these issues require national policy/legal guidance (if not international agreements), others are tactical in nature and can be fixed at lower levels while still others require technical innovations for new solutions. Let's look at what level the issues resides at.

At the International level we need agreements and processes to address attribution, supply chain, and legal issues. At the National level the government needs to set a consistent and interconnected policy/legal strategy, set up governance for standardization of taxonomy and metrics, publish our policy on deterrence, doctrine (with ROE), expand our development of the skilled work force we need through both training and exercises. To do this we have some organizations that should be the lead for specific missions:

- Congress would need to set the course for policy and legal statutes and assign/resource many of the roles discussed here.
- NIST would focus on taxonomy, metrics, auditing. They could establish standards for virtualization, cloud computing, data protection, insider threat protection, system integration, and mobile device management.

- DoD would develop doctrine with ROE. They would need to build ways to develop chain of trust and mission assurance for key command and control as well as weapon systems. They require a core of service members with cyber warrior skills through training and exercises. They are in a good position to address the classification processes, and stovepipe issues.
- DHS would focus on situational awareness, identity management, IDS/IPS, IPV6 implementation, and dealing with massive data. They would also be the lead for national program to increase risk awareness and developing the skilled workforce we need.
- DoS should be the lead for developing deterrence strategy and building international agreements.
- DoJ would focus on policy and legal enforcement of the laws we have.
- Organizations like Federally Funded Research and Development Centers and Defense Advanced Research Projects Agency (DARPA) would focus on resilience, chain of trust, attribution, and supply chain.

This assignment of challenges is extremely basic and does not represent a clear mapping of missions of the different agencies/organizations. We have left out players like Whitehouse CIO, CTO, and Cyber Security Coordinator as they don't control significant resources. We didn't include DoE who is working cybersecurity for smart grid technology. This list was just a sample of but reflects some of the intricacy involved with these issues. It is meant to be more of a starting point to allow everyone to weigh in on which issue belong to which organization. It is clear the current distributed and poorly coordinated effort is not proving to be effective enough to position the US to maintain their current level of influence in cyberspace. We need a national roadmap that assigns responsibility and resources to address these concerns.

Another way to categorize these challenges is to look at a rough timeline to solve them (understanding that resources determine if and when they will be solved). So, with no crystal ball, here is a prediction on some of the issues. In the next 5 years doctrine should be well established based on the current activity in DoD—though ROE may not be defined very well. There will also probably be new laws based on the number of bills in congress. Many technical issues like virtualization, cloud computing, identity management, data protection, massive data analysis, and situational awareness are all being heavily invested in and will see major improvements. Expect to see cyber being included in more exercises and cyber central exercises to become more common. IPv6 will force its way onto center stage and become a standard protocol—time will tell how much it solves. There are a lot of organizations, both inside the government and commercial that are working on metrics and auditing so we expect major improvements but it is doubtful there will be any global standards established.

For those cross walking all the issues we listed there are some we didn't talk about because we are unclear where they could fit so didn't try and make a prediction.

SUMMARY

The US faces multiple challenges today competing for limited resources but only one of them is woven throughout the rest and can be attacked by everyone from a lone individual to a nation state—cyberspace. There are a number of organizations trying to solve or profit from these issues but there is no critical mass to enable real progress on any of the key issues we have covered in this chapter. The national debate on cyber needs to determine what we must address as many of these issues have a long lead time to solve. We need a leap forward to introduce game changing technology or change the rules we play by with new policy or even morph the game board by a paradigm shift in the underlying infrastructure of the Internet.

REFERENCES

[1] Obama, President Barack. Remarks by the President on securing our nations cyber infrastructure. The White House web page [online]; May 29, 2009. <http://www.whitehouse.gov/the_press_office/Remarks-by-the-President-on-Securing-Our-Nations-Cyber-Infrastructure/>.

[2] IP3 National Cyber security R&D Challenges [online]. <http://www.thei3p.org/docs/publications/i3pnationalcybersecurity.pdf>.

[3] National Cyber leap year [online]. <http://www.nitrd.gov/leapyear/National_Cyber_Leap_Year_Background.pdf>.

[4] InfoSec's hard problem list [online]. <http://www.infosec-research.org/docs_public/20051130-IRC-HPL-FINAL.pdf>.

[5] Four grand challenges in trustworthy computing [online]. <http://www.cra.org/uploads/documents/resources/rissues/trustworthy.computing_.pdf>.

[6] DoE A scientific R&D approach to Cybersecurity [online]. <http://www.er.doe.gov/ascr/ProgramDocuments/Docs/CyberSecurityScienceDec2008.pdf>.

[7] Securing Cyberspace for 44th president report [online]. <http://csis.org/files/media/csis/pubs/081208_securingcyberspace_44.pdf>.

[8] <http://georgewbush-whitehouse.archives.gov/pcipb/>.

[9] Comprehensive National Cybersecurity Initiative (CNCI) focus areas [online]. <http://www.whitehouse.gov/cybersecurity/comprehensive-national-cybersecurity-initiative>.

[10] Obama's Cyberspace policy review [online].

[11] Staff JE. Cartwright ViceChairman Joint Chief of. Cyber Reference Library. National Security Cyberspace Institute, Inc. (NSCI) [online]. <http://nsci-va.com/CyberReferenceLib/2010-11-Joint%20Terminology%20for%20Cyberspace%20Operations.pdf>.

[12] General, Office of Inspector. DHS needs to improve the security posture of its Cybersecurity program systems. Department of Homeland Security [online]; August 2010. <http://www.dhs.gov/xoig/assets/mgmtrpts/OIG_10-111_Aug10.pdf>.

[13] General, Department of Homeland Security Office of Inspector. DHS. IG [online]; August 18, 2010. <http://www.dhs.gov/xoig/assets/mgmtrpts/OIG_10-111_Aug10.pdf>.

[14] NIST. Special Publications (800 Series) [online]; December 2010. <http://csrc.nist.gov/publications/PubsSPs.html>.

[15] Press, White House. Obama's cybersecurity progress [online]. <http://www.whitehouse.gov/administration/eop/nsc/cybersecurity/progressreports/july2010>.

[16] Wulf WA, Jones AK. Reflections on Cybersecurity. Sci Mag 2009;326(5955)

[17] DHS. DHS Library [online]; June 25, 2010. <http://www.dhs.gov/xlibrary/assets/ns_tic.pdf>.

[18] Stern-Dunyak A. Insider threats: countering Cyber Crime from within. MITRE [online]; October 2009. <http://www.mitre.org/news/digest/homeland_security/10_09/cyber_crime.html>.

[19] Lehren SS, Andrew W. Leaked cables offer raw look at US diplomacy. New York Times [online]; November 28, 2010. <http://www.nytimes.com/2010/11/29/world/29cables.html?_r=4&bl=&adxnnl=1&adxnnlx=1292778173-fMW1SzDCUGvclejwT3KnJA&pagewanted=all>.

[20] NIST. National Initiative for Cybersecurity Education (NICE) [online]; March 2010. <http://csrc.nist.gov/nice/>.

[21] NSA. National Centers of Academic Excellence [online]; December 17, 2010. <http://www.nsa.gov/ia/academic_outreach/nat_cae/index.shtml>.

[22] Alexander GKB. Statement to house committee on armed services. DoD [online]; September 23, 2010. <http://www.defense.gov/home/features/2010/0410_cybersec/docs/USCC%20Command%20Posture%20Statement_HASC_22SEP10_FINAL%20_OMB%20Approved_.pdf>.

[23] MITRE. Common Vulnerabilities and Exposures (CVE) [online, cited May 28, 2012]. <http://cve.mitre.org/cve/index.html>.

[24] CIO, Vivek Kundra US CIO homepage [online, cited May 28, 2012]. <http://www.cio.gov/>.

Where is Cyber Warfare Headed?

9

INFORMATION IN THIS CHAPTER:

- Technology-Based Trends
- Policy-Based Trends
- How to Defend in Today's Contested Virtual Environment

Technology has had impacts on warfare throughout history. Some caused a "Revolution in Military Affairs" (RMA), also known as "Military Technical Revolutions," like gunpowder, nuclear bombs, and space platforms. Others have caused paradigm shifts in organizational structures and doctrine such as airplanes, submarines, and machineguns. Some innovations have been transformational like stirrups, precision strike munitions, and radios. Some inventions were designed for the military while others like internal combustion engines, railways and information technology advances were leveraged by it. Some of these changes were incremental like the machinegun being a natural change to increase the rate of fire for rifles. Others reflect the concept of Black Swans [1] or Dragon Kings [2] where there was dramatic surprise about the change. Cyber warfare has undergone transformation under all these aspects of change.

Cyber warfare has undergone changes in what has been called, including Electronic Warfare, Information Superiority, Information Dominance, Network Centric Warfare, Information Warfare, Command, Control, Communications, Computers, Intelligence, Surveillance, and Reconnaissance (C4ISR), Hyperwar, Netwar, and Third Wave Warfare. These terms generally refer to conflicts in the cyber domain. Cyber is separate from other RMAs ongoing today in unmanned aerial vehicles (UAVs), nanotechnology, robotics, and biotechnology.

Cyber is built on a physical infrastructure but is unique in that it has a virtual component. It also is prone to more rapid shifts since software is developed at a much faster pace than hardware. Technology will continue to drive change in society, economies, and warfare. We will start by looking at some of the changes that have impacted the Internet in general.

As a baseline we have provided a timeline of the major cyber events along the cyber timeline (see Appendix 1). This is a good format to look for paradigm shifts in both security and threats as well as where we seem to be stuck in a paradox experiencing the same issues year after year. We will see that while at the time of an event many of us believed it to be significant, many seem to have had no long term impact. There are some major evolutionary events and a few with revolutionary impact. As a sample we would point to 1988 when the Morris worm should have been a wake-up call for security, but in 1999 we see the same thing when the Melissa virus hit, then again in 2004 when LoveLetter caused havoc. These show a pattern of the military and the IT industry ignoring the fundamental security issues that allowed these worms and viruses to spread. Some major (but still evolutionary) events in cyber conflicts are the 2004 SCADA attack on the Russian pipeline [3], 2007 attacks on Estonia [4], the 2008 Buckshot Yankee intrusions [5] and the cyber attacks against Georgia during conflict with Russia [6]. In 2010 we had Operation Aurora against Google [7] and Stuxnet SCADA [8] attacks. These events show an increasing use of cyber attacks with overtones of state sponsorship. In the revolutionary category there is ARPANET being stood up and social media exploding onto the net. These were events that created paradigm shifts in how we use the Internet and open up net threat vectors at the same time.

As we look at the potential threats, one way to categorize them is by the level of resources they commit [9]. There are some tier one nations that are committing billions of dollars to cyber warfare like the United States, China, and Russia. In McAfee's report "In the Crossfire Critical Infrastructure in the Age of Cyber War" executives from many nations, including many US allies, rank the United States as the country "of greatest concern" in the context of foreign cyber attacks, just ahead of China [10]. At the next level there are countries and non-nation state actors like criminal organizations investing millions of dollars in developing and employing cyber tools. Finally there are individual hackers or groups like Anonymous only spending thousands of dollars. Unfortunately unlike conventional weapons development the potential impact of these organizations can't be based on their resources alone. That said we will continue to see rapid increases in attack capability, many of which are designed to be stealth or classified.

Another way to categorize potential threats is how they impact aspects of national power. These would be based on evaluating impact of attack / defend / exploit capabilities across Diplomatic, Information, Military, and Economic (DIME) elements of national power. Typically discussions on warfare focus on armies, weapons, and leadership but in today's conflicts we are seeing more integration of all these capabilities. The US Secretary of Defense is talking about both cyber and the national debt today. DIME presents a solid way to evaluate the multiple aspects of Internet-based activities that can be part of cyber warfare. The impact of intellectual property theft can be looked at as economic warfare when you consider the aggregated damage to a nation—but what about the impact of cyber crime? This chapter will review where cyber warfare is going based on these elements, but in the end we must devise a national formula that will ensure we are ready for the next conflict based on something like Aggregation of capabilities + Innovations + Resources + Leadership = Strategic Advantage.

TECHNOLOGY-BASED TRENDS

The first technology that is changing the virtual landscape is cloud computing. For most companies running a network is a distraction and at some point it is natural to outsource tasks that are not part of the core business. Looking at a historical example of this, in the early days of electrical energy, manufacturing plants would run their own power plants, but as a common power grid became more reliable they eventually decided to move to it and go back to focusing on their core business. We are approaching that tipping point in the next few years with corporate networks and cloud computing where we see companies shift the capability to an external service with high expectations of reliability. As the cost, security, and reliability of cloud computing continue to increase it will become standard to get rid of the distraction of managing internal networks and outsource to the cloud. Use of the cloud will still need strong corporate governance and for some organizations (finance, military, intelligence community) just a few years ago it would never have been considered an acceptable risk, but today for most it will become standard. There are security advantages and disadvantages but again it is important to remember that the threat will target the place they can gain the most advantage or impact. Botnet builders love the idea of consolidating resources into one target; compromising one cloud provider would give them an instant botnet army. The Advanced Persistent Threat today has to break into multiple systems to find the information they are after, they also would love one target that has all the desired information. The military and critical infrastructures are moving to the cloud and it will impact the cyber landscape.

Another key issue is the number of mobile devices users are connecting to our networks so they can do their work and manage their personal life at the same time. People have laptops, smart phones, thumb drives and tablets to be more productive and few users think about security when they are using these mobile devices. Many users download applications to all these devices with no concern about the security or validity of the programs. There are also a lot of devices that are not necessarily mobile but are becoming connected to the Internet. Our cars can be remotely tracked, our houses will soon be able to be monitored to track our activities as our heating system and refrigerators become connected. While we think of the advantages, the threat is busy thinking of new "business models" to take advantage of them. If we are mad at our neighbor we can turn off their heating system when they leave for work in the winter. If we want to sell more tune ups we can remotely turn on the check engine light in the cars that use our garage. If we want to sell information on the people who live in Colorado Springs we can track their electricity usage and sell the information to companies that sell solar panels so they would know their best potential sales targets. Conversely, as Colorado Springs has five military forts/bases, you can track activity of both the installations and potentially key leaders based on energy consumption or other embedded devices.

Situational Awareness (SA) and Visualization are based on the correlation and fusion of data from multiple sources that enable decision making that is presented in an intuitive way to the units' leadership. Situational Awareness consists of functions like Continuous Monitoring (real time), Security Information and Event Management for correlation, Common Operational Picture (COP) for relevancy, and a Dashboard for visualization. Most of the current COPs / Dashboards fail to facilitate true risk posture understanding and provide information in a format that enables decisions. There are processes like situation awareness global assessment technique (SAGAT) [11] (Endsley, 1988, 1995b), situational awareness rating technique (SART) [11] (Taylor, 1990), and situation present awareness measurement (SPAM) [11] (Durso et al., 1998) that provide useful processes. The military needs to be able to understand both the impact to enterprise risk posture and mission capabilities of a network security event.

The number of Internet Protocol (IP) v4 addresses is running out quickly forcing new Internet sites to use IPv6. It is predicted, at the time of this writing, that there will be no more available within the next 18 months. As the Web pages on the Internet are divided into IPv4 vs. IPv6 there will be a number of security issues including no longer needing Network Address Translation (NAT) to extend IP addresses which will open up entire networks to discovery. Also most security tools we use today are not designed to operate over IPv6, and currently only a few skilled administrators and a limited number of vendors support IPv6. However, IPv6 has benefits such as, hacker scanning will become problematic as address space will be so much larger, Internet Protocol Security (IPsec) Encapsulating Security Payload (ESP) is designed-in, IPSec Authentication Header (AH) is embedded as well, we can have virtual private networks without tunnels and there is enhanced routing security. Countries like China are aggressively deploying IPv6 and will be ahead of the curve, which could give them a strategic advantage in capabilities and developing international standards. This change has been predicted for some time and it is hard to tell when we will hit the tipping point to move the majority of Web sites to IPv6.

Bring Your Own Device (BYOD) as the military and other organizations allow increasing numbers of employees to bring their personally owned devices to work, it will become more complex to implement enterprise security solutions. Allowing devices like data enabled phones, iPads, and laptops with different operating systems reduces cost of infrastructure but introduces more risk to security. Dale Meyerrose [12] points out this has been happening for years so in some ways this acknowledgement

---

NOTE

Cyber time is an interesting problem. We know 1 human year is roughly equal to 7 in a dog's lifespan. How do we measure cyber time? Some say we need to move at the speed of light (generally when talking about making decisions). Others that we need to move at the speed of need (mostly referring to acquisition). We have Moore's law that states the number of transistors on a chip will double about every 2 years. For how quickly things are changing in social media it would seem 1 cyber month is equal to 1 human year. For legal or regulatory practices it would be more like 1 cyber minute is equal to 1 year of legislative activity. One concern we face is we act like all these activities move at a constant speed rather than the relative speeds they really do.

of the practice could increase overall security. Soldiers are taking these devices onto the battlefield today. The impact to the military is now mission critical data could be on personal devices which are not under enterprise security.

Even if we do secure our networks we have "social networking" activities which open attack vectors that bypass our network security infrastructure. Most organizations are not putting the effort into training their staff on how to practice due care or diligence when on places like Facebook and Twitter so we believe this issue will continue to grow. The Air Force has put out an official policy on how to interact with social media as airmen posting about activities within a combat theater of operations could reveal mission sensitive information [13].

As the military considers threats to their capabilities, their reliance on publicly owned energy providers has started to be analyzed. Often referred to as Critical Infrastructure Protection (CIP)/Industrial control system (ICS)/Supervisory Control And Data Acquisition (SCADA) issues, the military has undertaken a program called Smart Power Infrastructure Demonstration for Energy Reliability and Security (SPIDERS) to make military installations energy self-sufficient [14]. On the commercial side, Jim Brenton [15], a Principal Regional Security Coordinator for Electric Reliability Council of Texas (ERCOT), talked about both the recent improvements driven by the North American Electric Reliability Corporation (NERC) CIP program and the energy sector's natural focus on reliability that is tested continuously by different extreme weather events around the country. All of the different critical infrastructures will continue to grow in importance as part of cyber conflicts.

Attack vector trends will continue to follow the most popular applications. As use of email grew, the threat used it to gain access. Today that is happening with social media and mobile devices. As we move forward there will naturally be new vectors for attack, some technical, others procedural but always following the latest technology trends as they normally have initially have immature security built in. Some good companies to follow to stay current are: iDefense, XForce, Dambala, iSight, and the annual CSI Computer Crime and Security Survey.

Cyber weapons like Stuxnet and Flame will continue to become more complex and capable. We will see more public doctrine and legal definitions built around the concept of cyber weapons. The US is investing in the development of these capabilities through projects like Plan X developed by Defense Advanced Research Projects Agency (DARPA) where "the Pentagon is turning to the private sector, universities, and even computer-game companies as part of an ambitious effort to develop technologies to improve its cyber warfare capabilities, launch effective attacks, and withstand the likely retaliation [16]." Expect the use of cyber weapons to continue to grow and become more categorized as to their level of impact which will be tied to the release authority.

A couple of new items of interest to security are biometric and nanotechnology trends. The trend toward biometrics is going to lead to new threats as their use grows. First there are no governing statutes protecting our biometric data today. Second, biometrics is not a silver bullet—the threat will eventually find ways to compromise it. Finally as we field these systems we will need to build analytics and security integrated into the design. If we use biometrics (perhaps to avoid some-one voting multiple times or registering for government aid under multiple names) we need to ensure it has been reviewed by folks who think like malicious hackers instead of engineers who think about how to make things work. The second is nano-technology where generally devices are sized from 1 to 100 nm. These devices can swarm to accomplish more complex tasks. The concerns revolve around building security into the devices upfront and losing control of the devices as they morph into new capabilities.

One final evolution to be considered is the change developing in defensive Security Operations Centers (SOC). Initially these incident response centers were focused on manually reviewing logs or output from standalone systems like Intrusions Detection Systems. Next they started correlation across multiple security devices to identify attacks. Now we are seeing a move toward what the military calls all-source intelligence where multiple types of intelligence feeds (technical and human) are integrated with a fusion cell. The new SOC will continue to drive toward the goal of predictive analysis but will need to take feeds from traditional Security Information and Event Management (SIEM) solutions and be able to integrate information from feeds like social media, cyber threat intelligence services, and user input. One example where this has been enabled was when the US had a single commander over both NSA and CyberCom facilitating collaboration across the two organizations.

POLICY-BASED TRENDS

There is an ongoing debate about whether there is a cyber war being waged today. There are clearly two sides to the argument. On the "cyberarmageddon" side the spokesperson is Mike McConnell, former Director of National Intelligence and currently a Senior Executive for a defense contractor, who wrote in Washington Post "The United States is fighting a cyber-war today, and we are losing. It's that simple [17]." On the "cyber war is hype" side Bruce Schneier wrote a Cable News Network (CNN) piece saying "We surely need to improve our cybersecurity. But words have meaning, and metaphors matter. There's a power struggle going on for control of our nation's cybersecurity strategy, and the National Security Agency (NSA) and Department of Defense (DoD) are winning. If we frame the debate in terms of war, if we accept the military's expansive cyberspace definition of "war," we feed our fears…If, on the other hand, we use the more measured language of cyber crime, we change the debate. Crime fighting requires both resolve and resources, but it's done within the context of normal life. We willingly give our police extraordinary powers of investigation and arrest, but we temper these powers with a judicial system and legal protections for citizens [18]." These arguments need to be weighed as they will determine how we approach and solve the cyber conflicts of today.

As we look at the progress achieved over the last couple of years there are two reports worth reviewing. The first is a report "Cybersecurity Two Years Later" by the Center for Strategic International Studies (CSIS) commission on cybersecurity for the 44th Presidency. It is a review of progress on the commission's original recommendations. Under the section "Prospects for Cybersecurity—2012" it states "Our review of the last 2 years found that there has been progress in almost all of the areas we identify as critical, but in no area has this progress been sufficient. The cybersecurity debate is stuck. Many of the solutions still advocated for cybersecurity are well past their sell-by date. Public-private partnerships, information sharing, and self-regulation, are remedies we have tried for more than a decade without success. We need new concepts and new strategies if we are to reduce the risks in cyberspace to the United States [19]." The second report is from a lesser known organization called National Security Cyberspace Institute called "Cybersecurity Report Card." It gave the Obama administration very average grades and most of the concern was on lack of timely progress on the goals set out in the Cybersecurity Report Card [20]. Both of these reports stress that while we are making progress it is very slow.

There is also an economic warfare aspect to what we are facing. In some ways the major cyber catastrophe that many newspapers predict has happened with the amount of data that has been stolen from militaries, governments, critical infrastructures, and commercial companies. The loss of Intellectual Property (patent, trade secrets, proprietary client data, business plans) is hard to measure and determine the scope of damage but attacks are rampant. One estimate put US losses of intellectual property and technology through cyber espionage at $240 billion. An estimate of German losses of intellectual property due to cyber espionage puts them at perhaps $20 billion [21]. Cyber crime is the second half of the economic equation. These two issues are eroding the economic powerbase the G8 countries like the United States enjoy today. Finally former Chairman of the Joint Chiefs of Staff, Adm. Mike Mullen, observed that one of the greatest threats to national security is our national debt [22]. This means the amount of money we can spend to improve cyber defensive capabilities will come under increasing pressure and many program in both the military and broader government may be delayed or cancelled.

We don't teach other countries how to build atomic-bombs in our universities but we do teach them everything we know about cyberspace. Most products related to cyber are not actively controlled by International Traffic in Arms Regulations (ITAR) as we don't have clear rules about what constitutes an export of a cyber capability that can be used as a weapon (classic example here is encryption). As the government (to include the military) has moved from driving technology to buying it they are now using standard commercial-off-the-shelf products many of which were programmed and built all around the world. Much of the research is now also being done overseas. So as we continue to realize and talk about how critical the cyber domain is to our national interests and what a central role it will play in any kind of conflict we are aggressively exporting everything about it.

The legal landscape for cyber is moving in two parallel directions today. First is the idea that private lawsuits will drive public law. The second is that Congress will enact laws to protect aspects of national critical infrastructure, privacy, and intellectual property [23]. There are a number of lawsuits and legislative initiatives ongoing today and there is no clear trend on what guiding principles will come from them.

At the same time there are commercial companies offering cyber services to support the military (see Blackwater principle in Chapter 3) and Law Enforcement Agencies to the point many organizations are outsourcing what was traditionally thought of as government employee-only work because of the lack of skills within the military. At the end of the day this is an international issue. Because the United States and China have developed technological capabilities in the cyber arena, the nations must work together to avoid misperception that could lead to a crisis, according to Defense Secretary Leon E. Panetta [25].

As we look at the leadership of most organizations today there is what we call the "wristwatch syndrome." Most of the people making decisions today were not raised around computers and think of them as support devices—not as the primary means of accomplishing the mission. They still wear their watch even though they have the time available on their cell phone because they have always worn a watch and don't need to change. The younger generation has never worn a watch and many have never had a camera that used film or know how to use a paper map. In fact one of the authors was at a simulation exercise and asked a young airman what they would do if they lost the network in the command center and was told, "we couldn't fly anymore." For the generation of military personal who used grease pencils (description can be found on Wikipedia for the younger readers) to track movement of entire divisions this attitude was unthinkable. So for the (let's not say older generation—we will go with Baby Boomers) baby boomers who are in charge today they many times don't think in terms of risk to mission when talking about the network. When the digital native generation takes over leadership of the terror groups plotting to attack the west they will default to remote attacks trying to use our mission control systems and critical infrastructure to be the central point of attack rather than a supporting function.

We have heard the term "Sputnik moment" [25] on the political stage lately. One of the institutions that came out of America's reaction to "losing the race to space" was DARPA [27]. DARPA has a cyber thrust designed to enable military systems and infrastructure to operate effectively in the presence of cyber attacks. Technologies that eliminate entire classes of vulnerabilities, that adapt immediately to evolutions or novel developments of the cyber threat, and that raise the cost of employing cyber technologies against US forces are the focus of this thrust. Also of interest are approaches to the development of cyber-based intelligence, surveillance and reconnaissance (ISR) capabilities, the integration of cyber technologies with communications and electronic warfare systems, and leverage of commercial advances with cyber technologies. They have a number of programs ongoing to include: Cyber Genome, Dynamic Quarantine of Computer-based Worm Attacks (DQW), Military Networking Protocol, National Cyber Range (NCR), Scalable Network Monitoring (SNM), Quantum Computing, Cyber Trust program, and Cyber Insider Threat (CINDER) [27]. These programs are aimed at keeping the US's technological edge. The question is, are they funded and able to move fast enough to do it.

There is a strong trend towards mergers and acquisitions in the cyber market. A few examples of this trend are HP acquired ArcSight (correlation), Fortify (code review), and Tipping Point (Intrusion Prevention Systems and Threat Management

Systems) to provide integrated cyber solutions. RSA acquired NetWitness (network detection and forensics), Archer (policy and compliance), envision (security incident management), and GreenPlum (database analytics) so they could provide single enterprise cybersecurity solution as well. Intel acquired Symantec to expand their product's capability. IBM has acquired a host of analytics companies focused on cyber and big data capabilities. Defense contracts like ManTech have expanded cyber capabilities by acquiring companies like HBGary (access to Computer Network Attack and Exploit customers) or in the case of Kratos who acquired Secure Info (certification and accreditation) and RTLogic (Satcom Cybersecurity) gain access into the cyber market. What is not clear is the impact of this trend. It could lead to a lack of open security solutions as more pure security companies disappear and their capabilities are offered as part of a larger package from a company or it could lead to better security products as the larger companies put more resources into growing the capabilities of the companies they have acquired. Finally as young cyber companies are acquired it reduces the possibility of the next Microsoft/Google/Facebook size company from impacting the security market in unexpected ways.

HOW TO DEFEND IN TODAY'S CONTESTED VIRTUAL ENVIRONMENT

Nation-level programs for short term maximum effect should focus on metrics and auditing. Today there are a number of efforts to help define a standard for cyber metrics. Some of the programs include: National Institute of Standards and Technology (NIST) Security Content Automation Protocol (SCAP) / SP 800-30 Risk Management Guide for Information Technology, Systems Common Criteria (ISO 18045 & ISO 15408), Operationally Critical Threat, Asset, and Vulnerability Evaluation (OCTAVE), and Control Objectives for Information and related Technology (COBIT). Traditional processes like Federal Information Security Management Act (FISMA) and DoD Information Technology Security Certification and Accreditation Process (DITSCAP) are transforming to continuous real time monitoring. MITRE has a "Making security measurable program" with Common Vulnerabilities and Exposures (CVE®) List, Common Platform Enumeration (CPE™) List, Common Weakness Scoring System (CWSS™), Common Weakness Risk Analysis Framework (CWRAF™), and Common Vulnerability Scoring System (CVSS) suite of tools. At the end of the day metrics should be specific, measurable, attainable, repeatable, and time-dependent (SMART) and enable decisions to ensure the security of the systems they monitor.

On the auditing side there is progress with Federal Risk and Authorization Management Program (FedRAMP) which is a government-wide program that provides a standardized approach to security assessment, authorization, and continuous monitoring for cloud products and services [28]. Some other useful standards are SANS' "Twenty Critical Security Controls for Effective Cyber Defense: Consensus Audit Guidelines," the SOC 1 Report (Service Organization Control Report that replaced American Institute of Certified Public Accountants SAS 70 standard) and ISO17799.

There are also industry specific standards like Health Insurance Portability and Accountability Act (HIPAA) for healthcare, Sarbanes-Oxley (SOX) for publicly traded companies, Gramm-Leach-Bliley (GLB) for financial institutions, and Payment Card Industry (PCI) for credit card data security. Both metrics and real time audits are key to develop a safer cyber landscape.

We are facing cyber fatigue today. It seems like there is a story about cyber crime or war in the news every week. At some point it is hard to maintain enthusiasm for fixing cybersecurity. Here is a sample conversation:

CEO—*If we give you all the money you want to build the best cybersecurity possible could you guarantee our systems would be secure?*
CISO—*Nope, there could be a zero day exploit that we cannot protect against.*
CEO—*Then why should we invest more than the absolute minimum?*

When we look at the cost and constant impact that is going on around us it maybe we need to determine the "cost of doing business [29]."

When looking to protect your organization, the key principles to build on are: shaping the behavior of the users (i.e. using care when opening attachments) so they don't assume their system is secure. Building defense-in-depth and principle of least privilege into the network design. Managing identities to enforce authenticate (who they are), authorization (what they can access), and auditing (logging what they did). It should be built on Safety, Risk Management, and Mission Assurance. When looking to protect yourself, the principles are similar: remember the computer is not a trusted environment anymore so stop thinking it is safe when you sit down and log in. Things like email attachments (i.e. PDF or Power Point), games, Web sites, and even thumb drives can be attack vectors. First don't trust anything where you cannot validate the source. Make sure the firewall, anti-virus, and programs like spy-ware detectors are up to date and running. A good practice is to periodically manually update the AV and run a scan. Make sure the operating system and application are current with all patches. Check the known hash (digital fingerprint) of software you are downloading. Most importantly BACKUP all essential data on an external hard drive.

For the younger generation there is a careful balance between access and teaching them to operate in the cyberspace. We need them to be competitive and want them to interested in building the next generation of cybersecurity capabilities. There are programs like CyberPatriot program for JROTC and high school students, National Collegiate Cyber Defense Competition (CCDC) and US military Cyber Defense Exercise (CDX) for college level competition that will help them gain the skills to become the next generation of cyber security leaders.

SUMMARY

So as we look at the different eras; Stone age, Bronze age, Iron age, Agricultural age, Industrial age, Information age, Space age, and now Digital age it is clear that technology has been a large driver in our progress. The pace of change has increased over time and continues to accelerate almost exponentially. The domains of war have gone from kinetic to analog to digital and are now enmeshed with our baseline society infrastructure. There are Evolutionary (wiki leaks, Stuxnet) vs. Revolutionary (social media) challenges coming and we need to have a process to address them at the speed of need.

We must pull from adjacent disciplines such as cultural experts like Toffler (three key drivers of change that are powerfully shaping the future of businesses and governments are innovation, sustainability, and adaptability) [30] and change management experts like Dr. John Kotter (studies have proven that 70% of all major change efforts in organizations fail) [31]. to help us organize the right answer but in the end we must devise a formula that will make sure we are ready for the next challenge—whether we call it a war or not.

Finally it is key to establish the roles and responsibilities for cyber conflicts. If this is a war then it belongs to the military, if it is espionage it belongs to the intelligence agencies, if it is a national security issue it belongs to Department of Homeland Security (DHS). "This is a turf war, The Constitution doesn't allow for idiocy. You either make DHS do their job or you find another way." said James Cartwright, the retired US Marine Corps general who stepped down as vice chairman of the Joint Chiefs of Staff in August and is now with the Center for Strategic and International Studies. The idea of DoD, in the form of US Cyber Command (CYBERCOM), assisting when it comes to attacks against private entities runs into potential legal problems, said Dale Meyerrose, former associate director of National Intelligence and founder of the Meyerrose Group. "It's against the law," he said. "We sometimes forget that the United States military does not protect the United States except in a very gross aggregate sense. The United States military does not operate within the borders of the United States. What they're calling for is a redefinition of that role [32]."

As we move forward into the cyber domain of warfare there will continue to be national and international issues around doctrine, legal principals and generally accepted use of cyberspace as a battle space. For now, understand there are active cyber conflicts across the national elements of power and continued need for skilled practitioners and capabilities to deal with them.

REFERENCES

[1] Taleb, Nassim. NY Times First Chapters [online]; April 22, 2007. <http://www.nytimes.com/2007/04/22/books/chapters/0422-1st-tale.html>.

[2] Didier Sornette Dragon-Kings, Black Swans and the Prediction of Crises [online]; August 2009 <http://www.uvm.edu/~pdodds/files/papers/others/2009/sornette2009a.pdf>.

[3] Reed Thomas C. At the Abyss: an insider's history of the cold war. NY: Ballantine; 2005.

[4] Davis Joshua. Hackers take down the most wired country in Europe [online]; August 21, 2007. <http://www.wired.com/politics/security/magazine/15-09/ff_estonia?currentPage=all>.

[5] Jackson William. The cyberattack that awakened the Pentagon [online]; August 25, 2010. <http://gcn.com/articles/2010/08/25/dod-cyberdefense-strategy-082510.aspx>.

[6] Krebs Brian. 'Russian Hacker Forums Fueled Georgia Cyber Attacks [online]; October 16, 2008. <http://voices.washingtonpost.com/securityfix/2008/10/report_russian_hacker_forums_f.html>.

[7] Zetter Kim. Google Hack attack was ultra sophisticated, new details show [online]; January 14, 2010. <http://www.wired.com/threatlevel/2010/01/operation-aurora/>.

[8] Zetter Kim. How digital detectives deciphered stuxnet, the most menacing malware in History [online]; July 11, 2011. <http://www.wired.com/threatlevel/2011/07/how-digital-detectives-deciphered-stuxnet/>.

[9] Interview with James Gosler Sandia Fellow; May 26, 2012.

[10] McAfee in the crossfire-critical infrastructure in the age of cyber war [online]; February 2010. <http://www.mcafee.com/us/resources/reports/rp-in-crossfire-critical-infrastructure-cyber-war.pdf>.

[11] Paul Salmon*, Prof Stanton Neville, Dr Walker Guy & Dr Green Damian. Situation awareness measurement: a review of applicability for C4i environments [online]. <http://bura.brunel.ac.uk/bitstream/2438/1422/1/Situation_awareness_measurement_Salmon_et_al.pdf>.

[12] Interview with Major General (Retired) Dale Meyerrose on May 29, 2012.

[13] US Air Force 'New Media and The Air Force [online]; 2009. <http://www.af.mil/shared/media/document/AFD-091210-037.pdf>.

[14] Sandia National Lab SPIDERS [online]; February 2012. <http://energy.sandia.gov/?page_id=2781>.

[15] Interview with side Jim Brenton 17 a Principal Regional Security Coordinator for Electric Reliability Council of Texas (ERCOT) on June 8, 2012.

[16] Ellen Nakashima The Washington Post With Plan X, Pentagon seeks to spread U.S. military might to cyberspace [online]; May 30. <http://www.washingtonpost.com/world/national-security/with-plan-x-pentagon-seeks-to-spread-us-military-might-to-cyberspace/2012/05/30/gJQAEca71U_story.html>.

[17] McMonnell Mike. Washington Post. Outlook & Opinions [online]; February 28, 2010. <http://www.washingtonpost.com/wp-dyn/content/article/2010/02/25/AR2010022502493.html>.

[18] Schneier Bruce. Threat of "Cyberwar" Has Been Hugely Hyped. CNN [online]; July 7, 2010. <http://edition.cnn.com/2010/OPINION/07/07/schneier.cyberwar.hyped/>.

[19] Headline News 'White House Scores Low on Cybersecurity Report Card' [online]; January 25, 2011. <http://csis.org/publication/cybersecurity-two-years-later>.

[20] CSIS Commission on Cybersecurity for the 44th Presidency Cybersecurity Two Years Later [online]; January 31, 2011. <http://www.infosecisland.com/blogview/11350-White-House-Scores-Low-on-Cybersecurity-Report-Card.html>.

[21] James A. Lewis House of Representatives Committee on Oversight and Government Reform Subcommittee on National Security, Homeland Defense and Foreign Operations. "Cybersecurity: Assessing the Immediate Threat to the United States" [online]; May 25, 2011. <http://oversight.house.gov/wp-content/uploads/2012/01/5-25-11_Lewis_NatSec_Testimony.pdf>.

[22] David Langstaff Leading CEO asks: do we dare protect national security on a shoestring? [online]; June 20, 2012. <http://washingtontechnology.com/Articles/2012/06/20/Langstaff-commentary.aspx?p=1>.

[23] Interview with Douglas DePeppe Principal at i2IS Cyberspace, Solutions June 1, 2012.

[24] Cheryl Pellerin US, China Must Work Together on Cyber, Panetta Says [online]; May 7, 2012. <http://www.defense.gov/news/newsarticle.aspx?id=116235>.

[25] Wilson Scott. What's a 'Sputnik moment'? washingtonpost.com [online]; January 25, 2011. <http://voices.washingtonpost.com/44/2011/01/whats-a-sputnik-moment.html>.

[26] DARPA History. [online, cited January 17, 2011]. <http://www.darpa.mil/About/History/History.aspx>.

[27] DARPA. Strategic Technology Office [online, cited January 17, 2011]. <http://www.darpa.mil/Our_Work/I2O/Programs/>.

[28] GSA FEDRAMP [online]. <http://www.gsa.gov/portal/catcgory/102371>.

[29] Interview with John Peschtore VP / Distinguished Analysis at Gartner; May 30, 2012.

[30] Associates, Toffler. Technology and Innovation 2025. [online, cited January 17, 2010]. <http://www.toffler.com/our-thinking/other-publications.html>.

[31] Kotter Dr. John. The 8 step process [online, cited January 17, 2011]. <http://www.kotterinternational.com/kotterprinciples/changesteps>.

[32] Fryer-Biggs Zachary. 'Debate slows new US cyber rules [online]; May 7, 2012. <http://www.defensenews.com/article/20120507/DEFREG02/305070004/Debate-Slows-New-U-S-Cyber-Rules>.

Index

Printed and bound by CPI Group (UK) Ltd, Croydon, CR0 4YY

03/10/2024

01040322-0010